COOKIES
BROWNIES
MUFFINS *and* MORE

In all Rodale cookbooks, our mission is to provide delicious and nutritious recipes. Our recipes also meet the standards of the Rodale Test Kitchen for dependability, ease, practicality, and, most of all, great taste. To give us your comments, call (800) 848-4735.

RODALE'S
New
Classics™

COOKIES
BROWNIES
MUFFINS *and* MORE

By Anne Egan

RODALE

Cover and Interior Designer: Richard Kershner

Cover Photographer: Lisa Koenig

Cover Food Stylist: Diane Vezza

Interior Photos: Rodale Images

Front Cover Recipes: Double Chocolate–Peanut Cookies (page 18), Cranberry Macaroons (page 27), Marbled Brownies (page 59), Iced Butterscotch Brownies (page 66), Orange–Poppy Seed Muffins (page 97)

Library of Congress Cataloging-in-Publication Data

Egan, Anne.

    Cookies, brownies, muffins, and more / by Anne Egan.

        p.   cm. — (Rodale's new classics)

    Includes index.

    ISBN 1–57954–285–9   paperback

    1. Cookies.   2. Muffins.   3. Confectionery I. Title.

    TX772 .E34   2000

    641.8'654—dc21   00–009099

Distributed to the book trade by St. Martin's Press

2   4   6   8   10   9   7   5   3   1   paperback

Visit us on the Web at www.rodalecookbooks.com, or call us toll-free at (800) 848-4735.

RODALE
WE INSPIRE AND ENABLE PEOPLE TO IMPROVE
THEIR LIVES AND THE WORLD AROUND THEM

HOMEMADE FIG BARS
Page 17

BROWNIE CAKE SQUARES
Page 65

Contents

BLUEBERRY MUFFINS
Page 71

FRUIT-STUDDED COFFEE CAKE
Page 105

Introduction

Simple, sublime, and satisfying—cookies, brownies, muffins, quick breads, and cakes are favorites in every family. The beauty of these sweet treats is that typically, they are simple to prepare. I have taken traditional recipes and made them even faster and easier. As a matter of fact, these homemade recipes are just as fast as a packaged mix. Most of the ingredients needed are already in your cupboard. The good news is that the taste is so superior, you'll wonder why you ever bothered with a mix. The bonus: They're a fraction of the cost.

Rodale's New Classics is about keeping your life simple while enjoying the process of cooking and baking. For me, baking is an enjoyable, relaxing activity. The key is in knowing the tricks that make baking easy and effortless. Besides the enjoyment I

gain from baking, feeding my family the very best is the reason I choose to bake from scratch.

But don't do all the work yourself, even if it is fun. This type of quick baking is the perfect way to introduce your children to the kitchen. Not only will they love to prepare the dough (no snitching if it contains raw eggs), shape the cookies, or decorate the finished product but they will also enjoy every bite of the fruits of their labor.

Here are the baking basics that make cookies, brownies, muffins, quick breads, and cakes so easy to prepare.

Baking Pans and Sheets

Baking sheets come in a variety of styles. Black trays absorb heat and are used to crisp the bottom of cookies. Shiny sheets reflect heat and are used when a more delicate crust is required. If you have problems with cookies burning, try the air-cushioned sheets that help prevent overbaking. Some recipes call for lining sheets with parchment paper, which prevents sticking without added fat.

Typical baking pan sizes are 13" x 9", 8" x 8", and 9" round. Use metal pans with straight sides whenever possible. If you are baking with glass pans, be sure to reduce the oven temperature by 25°F.

Greasing sheets and pans is essential for many recipes to prevent the baked goods from sticking. Some recipes call for ungreased sheets because there is enough fat in the recipe to prohibit sticking.

The fastest way to grease the sheets and pans is to coat them with cooking spray. If a recipe says to grease and flour, you may sift the flour over the spray and then respray, if called for. If you prefer to grease with butter or shortening, using a pastry brush is the simplest way to do this.

All the muffin recipes in this book make 12 muffins. However, you may want to make jumbo muffins by filling the cups three-quarters of the way full and making only 10 muffins. Whenever you do not fill all 12 muffin cups, add hot water to any unfilled cups to keep the heat even in the pan and prevent the empty cups from burning.

Preparing the Batter

These simple baked items are prepared in a two-step process. The first step is to incorporate the dry ingredients. These are usually combined in a medium bowl. I like to use a whisk to be sure that the leavening agent (baking powder, baking soda, or cream of tartar) and the salt are evenly distributed within the flour. If you do not have a whisk, a fork works fine.

The second step is to combine the wet ingredients. If using butter, it is creamed with the sugar and then mixed with the remaining wet ingredients such as eggs and milk. The recipes in this book call for butter because I believe it produces the best-tasting baked goods and is healthier than margarine. If you prefer to bake with margarine, however, be sure to use stick margarine.

If a recipe calls for oil, it is combined with the other liquid ingredients. Use a whisk or wooden spoon to combine these ingredients.

Allow the refrigerated ingredients to come to room temperature. This will make mixing easier and help ensure that each ingredient is thoroughly incorporated.

When measuring a dry ingredient, especially flour, spoon it lightly into the measuring cup and then level with a metal spatula or knife.

Liquid should be poured into a glass liquid measuring cup. For accuracy, always read the measurement at eye level.

When measuring sticky ingredients such as honey or molasses, measure the oil in the recipe first, then use the same measure for the sticky item. It will slide right out. If no oil is in the recipe, spray the measuring spoon or cup with cooking spray.

Baking

Always preheat the oven to ensure even baking and browning. An easy way to remember is to turn on the oven when you begin assembling the ingredients. The oven should be the correct temperature by the time the batter is mixed.

Cookies are often baked in several batches. Place cookie dough on

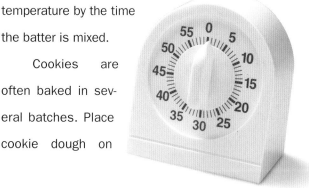

cool baking sheets because it will spread on hot ones.

Since cookies bake so quickly, leaving them in the oven for even a minute longer than required will make them dry and tough. In addition, cookies continue cooking for a minute or two after they're out of the oven, so remove them just before you think that they are done. They will be lightly browned at this point. Drop and rolled cookies will also have firm edges. Bar cookies are done when the edges appear dry and begin to pull away from the sides of the pan.

Here are two ways to tell if brownies are done: They will begin to pull away from the edges of the pan, and a wooden pick inserted in the center will come out with moist crumbs on it.

Muffins, quick breads, and cakes are done when a wooden pick inserted in the center comes out clean.

Storing

For best flavor and texture, store different kinds of cookies and bars in separate containers. If crisp cookies become soft, heat in a 300°F oven for 3 to 5 minutes to recrisp. To keep soft cookies from hardening, add a piece of bread or apple to the container; replace it often.

To store brownies for a few days, leave them in the pan and cover it with foil or plastic wrap.

Muffins, quick breads, and cakes should be stored in air-tight containers or resealable food storage bags.

All of these baked items freeze well. Place them in air-tight plastic containers for up to 3 months.

Whether light and delicate or rich and dense, there is nothing quite as delicious as fresh-from-the-oven baked goods. This book is filled with simple, quick recipes that I hope you and your family will delight in baking and eating. Enjoy!

INCREDIBLE
COOKIES

Chocolate Chunk Cookies

1½ cups unbleached all-purpose flour

½ teaspoon baking soda

¼ teaspoon salt

6 ounces bittersweet chocolate

½ cup butter, at room temperature

⅓ cup packed brown sugar

⅓ cup granulated sugar

1 egg

2 teaspoons vanilla extract

Be sure to scoop up all the chocolate crumbs that accumulate from chopping the chocolate. These tiny bits increase the chocolate density of the cookies.

Preheat the oven to 375°F.

In a medium bowl, combine the flour, baking soda, and salt. Coarsely chop the chocolate, reserving all the chunks and chocolate crumbs.

In a large bowl, with an electric mixer on medium speed, beat the butter, brown sugar, and granulated sugar for 3 minutes, or until light and fluffy. Beat in the egg and vanilla extract. Beat in the flour mixture, a little at a time, until well-blended. Stir in the chopped chocolate.

Drop by tablespoonfuls about 2" apart onto ungreased baking sheets. Bake for 10 minutes, or until golden brown. Cool on a rack for 2 minutes. Remove to the rack to cool completely.

Makes 36

Per cookie: 84 calories, 2 g protein, 11 g carbohydrates, 5 g fat, 14 mg cholesterol, 1 g fiber, 65 mg sodium

Best-Ever Mint Chip Cookies

2¼ cups unbleached all-purpose flour

¾ teaspoon baking soda

½ teaspoon salt

1 cup butter, at room temperature

1 cup packed brown sugar

½ cup granulated sugar

2 eggs

1 teaspoon vanilla extract

1 package (10 ounces) mint chocolate chips

Deliciously crisp and refreshingly minty—both describe these traditional drop cookies. For smaller cookies, drop by the teaspoonfuls and bake for a minute or two less.

Preheat the oven to 375°F.

In a medium bowl, combine the flour, baking soda, and salt.

In a large bowl, with an electric mixer on medium speed, beat the butter, brown sugar, and granulated sugar for 3 minutes, or until light and fluffy. Beat in the eggs and vanilla extract. Beat in the flour mixture, a little at a time, until well-blended. Stir in the chips.

Drop by tablespoonfuls about 2" apart onto ungreased baking sheets. Bake for 10 minutes, or until golden brown. Cool on a rack for 2 minutes. Remove to the rack to cool completely.

Makes 60

Per cookie: 93 calories, 1 g protein, 12 g carbohydrates, 5 g fat, 16 mg cholesterol, 1 g fiber, 73 mg sodium

Homemade Fig Bars

18 dried figs, stems removed (about 10 ounces)

¾ cup raisins

1½ cups + 3–4 tablespoons water

⅓ cup granulated sugar

¼ teaspoon ground cardamom

1¼ cups whole grain pastry flour

1 cup oat bran

¼ cup packed brown sugar

¼ teaspoon salt

½ cup butter, cut into small pieces

Here, naturally sweet dried figs are wrapped in a tender crust for a store-bought look-alike that's really a healthy treat.

Preheat the oven to 400°F. Grease baking sheets.

Coarsely chop the figs and place in a food processor. Add the raisins and pulse until fairly smooth. Place in a medium saucepan. Add the 1½ cups water, granulated sugar, and cardamom. Bring to a boil over medium-high heat. Reduce the heat to medium-low and cook, stirring occasionally, for 15 minutes, or until the mixture thickens. Remove from the heat.

In a food processor, combine the flour, oat bran, brown sugar, and salt. Process briefly. Add the butter. Process until well-combined. Slowly add the remaining water, 1 tablespoon at a time, until the mixture forms a ball.

Turn the mixture onto a floured surface. Divide in half. Using a rolling pin, roll into 2 rectangles, each 3" wide and 24" long. Spoon half of the fig mixture down the center of each rectangle. Carefully fold the sides over the fig mixture, pinching the edges together in the center. Cut into 1½"-long pieces. Place on the prepared baking sheets.

Bake for 10 minutes, or until lightly browned. Cool on a rack for 2 minutes. Remove to the rack to cool completely.

Makes 26
Per bar: 127 calories, 2 g protein, 23 g carbohydrates, 2 g fat, 10 mg cholesterol, 3 g fiber, 64 mg sodium

Double Chocolate–Peanut Cookies

2¼ cups unbleached all-purpose flour

⅔ cup unsweetened cocoa powder

1 teaspoon baking soda

1¼ cups butter, at room temperature

⅔ cup packed brown sugar

⅔ cup granulated sugar

2 eggs

1 teaspoon vanilla extract

1 teaspoon warm water

1 cup peanut butter chips

1 cup white chocolate chips

These yummy chocolate treats are studded with peanut butter and white chocolate bits. If white chocolate isn't your passion, milk chocolate would be just as delicious.

Preheat the oven to 350°F.

In a medium bowl, combine the flour, cocoa, and baking soda.

In a large bowl, with an electric mixer on medium speed, beat the butter, brown sugar, and granulated sugar for 3 minutes, or until light and fluffy. Beat in the eggs, vanilla extract, and water. Beat in the flour mixture, a little at a time, until well-blended. Stir in the peanut butter and chocolate chips.

Drop by tablespoonfuls about 2" apart onto ungreased baking sheets. Bake for 10 minutes, or until golden brown. Cool on a rack for 2 minutes. Remove to the rack to cool completely.

Makes 60

Per cookie: 128 calories, 3 g protein, 14 g carbohydrates, 8 g fat, 19 mg cholesterol, 1 g fiber, 81 mg sodium

Nuts and Candy Cookies

1¼ cups rolled oats
1 cup unbleached all-purpose flour
3 tablespoons unsweetened cocoa powder
1 teaspoon baking powder
½ teaspoon baking soda
¼ teaspoon salt
½ cup butter, at room temperature
½ cup packed brown sugar
½ cup granulated sugar
1 egg
1 teaspoon vanilla extract
1 cup candy-coated chocolate pieces
½ cup coarsely chopped walnuts

Not your run-of-the-mill oat cookies. These drop goodies are laced with walnuts and colorful candy. Perfect for parties and spur-of-the-moment treats.

Preheat the oven to 350°F. Grease baking sheets.

In a medium bowl, combine the oats, flour, cocoa powder, baking powder, baking soda, and salt.

In a large bowl, with an electric mixer on medium speed, beat the butter, brown sugar, and granulated sugar for 3 minutes, or until light and fluffy. Beat in the egg and vanilla extract. Beat in the flour mixture, a little at a time, until well-blended. Stir in the candy-coated chocolate pieces and nuts.

Drop by rounded tablespoonfuls about 2" apart onto the prepared baking sheets. Bake for 8 minutes, or until brown. Cool on a rack for 2 minutes. Remove to the rack to cool completely.

Makes 80
Per cookie: 58 calories, 1 g protein, 9 g carbohydrates, 3 g fat, 7 mg cholesterol, 1 g fiber, 37 mg sodium

Cherry-Oatmeal Cookies

3 cups rolled oats

1½ cups unbleached all-purpose flour

1 teaspoon ground cinnamon

¼ teaspoon ground cardamom

½ teaspoon baking soda

¼ teaspoon salt

1 cup butter, at room temperature

¾ cup packed brown sugar

¾ cup granulated sugar

2 eggs

½ teaspoon almond extract

2 cups dried cherries, chopped

Dried cherries give these delightful cookies pizzazz. Try substituting dried cranberries or raisins for a change of pace.

Preheat the oven to 350°F.

In a medium bowl, combine the oats, flour, cinnamon, cardamom, baking soda, and salt.

In a large bowl, with an electric mixer on medium speed, beat the butter, brown sugar, and granulated sugar for 3 minutes, or until light and fluffy. Beat in the eggs and almond extract. Beat in the oat mixture, a little at a time, until well-blended. Stir in the cherries.

Drop by rounded tablespoonfuls about 2" apart onto ungreased baking sheets. Bake for 10 minutes, or until golden brown. Cool on a rack for 2 minutes. Remove to the rack to cool completely.

Makes 48

Per cookie: 167 calories, 3 g protein, 25 g carbohydrates, 7 g fat, 20 mg cholesterol, 1 g fiber, 72 mg sodium

Easy Almond Bites

2½ cups unbleached all-purpose flour

½ teaspoon cream of tartar

½ teaspoon baking soda

¼ teaspoon salt

1 cup butter, at room temperature

½ cup confectioners' sugar

½ cup granulated sugar

1 egg

1 teaspoon almond extract

1 tablespoon water

Chocolate sprinkles

Butter, almond, and chocolate—this trio of melt-in-your mouth flavors is a hit in a tender cookie anytime, anywhere.

In a medium bowl, combine the flour, cream of tartar, baking soda, and salt.

In a large bowl, with an electric mixer on medium speed, beat the butter, confectioners' sugar, and granulated sugar for 3 minutes, or until light and fluffy. Beat in the egg, almond extract, and water. Beat in the flour mixture, a little at a time, until well-blended. Cover with plastic wrap and refrigerate for 1 hour, or until easy to handle.

Preheat the oven to 350°F. Shape the dough into 1" balls and roll in the sprinkles. Place about 2" apart on ungreased cookie sheets. Bake for 9 minutes, or until set. Cool on a rack for 2 minutes. Remove to the rack to cool completely.

Makes 40

Per cookie: 107 calories, 2 g protein, 13 g carbohydrates, 6 g fat, 19 mg cholesterol, 0 g fiber, 82 mg sodium

Scotch Bars

2 cups unbleached all-purpose flour

1 teaspoon baking soda

½ teaspoon salt

½ cup butter, at room temperature

1 cup packed brown sugar

2 eggs

1 teaspoon vanilla extract

1½ cups butterscotch-flavored chips

1 cup coarsely chopped pecans

Confectioners' sugar

For dessert on the double, give these easy-to-assemble bars a whirl. They take just 20 minutes to bake and get their name from butterscotch chips.

Preheat the oven to 350°F. Grease a 13" x 9" baking pan.

In a medium bowl, combine the flour, baking soda, and salt.

In a large bowl, with an electric mixer on medium speed, beat the butter and brown sugar for 3 minutes, or until light and fluffy. Beat in the eggs and vanilla extract. Beat in the flour mixture, a little at a time, until well-blended. Stir in the chips and pecans.

Spread in the prepared pan. Bake for 20 minutes, or until golden brown. Cool completely in the pan on a rack. Dust with the confectioners' sugar. Cut into 1½" squares.

Makes 48

Per bar: 105 calories, 2 g protein, 14 g carbohydrates, 6 g fat, 15 mg cholesterol, 1 g fiber, 65 mg sodium

Orange Drop Cookies

1⅓ cups unbleached all-purpose flour

½ teaspoon baking powder

⅛ teaspoon baking soda

¼ teaspoon salt

¼ cup butter, at room temperature

2 tablespoons cream cheese

1 egg

½ cup sugar

1 tablespoon grated orange peel

1 teaspoon orange extract

Orange peel as well as orange extract gives these light cookies their unmistakable and delicious citrus tang.

Preheat the oven to 350°F. Line baking sheets with parchment paper.

In a medium bowl, combine the flour, baking powder, baking soda, and salt.

In a large bowl, with an electric mixer on medium speed, beat the butter, cream cheese, egg, sugar, orange peel, and orange extract for 3 minutes, or until light. The mixture will appear curdled. Beat in the flour mixture, a little at a time, until well-blended.

Drop by teaspoonfuls about 2" apart onto the prepared baking sheets. Bake for 10 minutes, or until the edges are golden. Remove, with the paper, to a rack. Let cool 10 for minutes and peel off the paper.

Makes 30

Per cookie: 55 calories, 1 g protein, 8 g carbohydrates, 3 g fat, 13 mg cholesterol, 1 g fiber, 55 mg sodium

Apple Pinwheel Cookies

1 cup chopped dried apples

¾ cup apple juice

½ teaspoon ground cinnamon

1 tablespoon lemon juice

2½ cups unbleached all-purpose flour

1 teaspoon baking powder

¼ teaspoon salt

¾ cup butter, at room temperature

1 cup sugar

2 eggs

1 teaspoon lemon extract

Most pinwheel cookies sport two flavors of dough, such as chocolate and vanilla. But these innovative creations swirl together lemon dough and a thick cinnamon-apple mixture.

In a medium saucepan, combine the apples, apple juice, cinnamon, and lemon juice. Bring to a boil over medium-high heat. Reduce the heat to low, cover, and simmer for 35 minutes, or until the apples are tender and most of the juice has been absorbed. Let cool slightly. Mash with a fork. Set aside.

Meanwhile, in a medium bowl, combine the flour, baking powder, and salt.

In a large bowl, with an electric mixer on medium speed, beat the butter and sugar for 3 minutes, or until light and fluffy. Beat in the eggs and lemon extract. Beat in the flour mixture a little at a time until well-blended. Cover and refrigerate for at least 1 hour.

Divide the dough in half. On a floured surface, roll each half into an 11" x 7" rectangle. Spread half of the apple mixture over each rectangle, leaving ½" edges. Starting at a long side, roll up tightly. Pinch to seal. Wrap in plastic wrap and refrigerate for at least 4 hours, or until firm.

Preheat the oven to 375°F. Cut rolls into ½" thick slices. Arrange on ungreased baking sheets. Bake for 10 minutes, or until light brown. Cool on a rack for 2 minutes. Remove to the rack to cool completely.

Makes 50
Per cookie: 86 calories, 2 g protein, 11 g carbohydrates, 4 g fat, 17 mg cholesterol, 1 g fiber, 54 mg sodium

Cranberry Macaroons

1   can (14 ounces) sweetened condensed milk

1   package (14 ounces) shredded coconut

1   cup dried cranberries

¾   cup unbleached all-purpose flour

¾   cup slivered almonds, toasted

¾   cup chocolate-covered raisins

1   teaspoon almond extract

Traditional macaroons feature almonds or coconut. These scrumptious goodies have both plus cranberries and chocolate-covered raisins for added visual and flavor appeal.

Preheat the oven to 350°F. Grease baking sheets.

In a large bowl, stir together the condensed milk, coconut, cranberries, flour, almonds, chocolate-covered raisins, and almond extract. Drop by tablespoons onto the prepared baking sheets.

Bake for 14 minutes, or until lightly golden. Cool on a rack for 2 minutes. Remove to the rack to cool completely.

Makes 40

Per cookie: 127 calories, 3 g protein, 15 g carbohydrates, 7 g fat, 4 mg cholesterol, 2 g fiber, 17 mg sodium

Almond Macaroons

1½ cups ground toasted
almonds
¼ cup flour
¼ teaspoon salt
3 egg whites
½ teaspoon almond extract
1 cup sugar

*These chewy bites are packed with a lively almond flavor and texture.
Serve for afternoon tea or a light dessert.*

Preheat the oven to 325°F. Line a baking sheet with parchment paper.

In a small bowl, combine the almonds, flour, and salt.

In a large bowl, with an electric mixer on high speed, beat the egg whites until soft peaks form. Add the almond extract. Gradually beat in the sugar, ¼ cup at a time, until stiff peaks form.

Fold the almond mixture into the egg whites.

Drop the batter by heaping teaspoons 2" apart onto the prepared sheet.

Bake for 14 minutes, or until light brown. Cool on a rack for 3 minutes.

Slide the parchment paper off the pan onto the rack to cool completely. Peel off the paper.

Makes 36

*Per cookie: 57 calories, 1 g protein, 7 g carbohydrates, 3 g fat,
0 mg cholesterol, 1 g fiber, 21 mg sodium*

Toasted Pecan Cookies

½ cup + 3 tablespoons pecans, toasted and finely chopped
1 cup rolled oats
1 cup packed brown sugar
2 tablespoons unbleached all-purpose flour
3 tablespoons butter, melted
1 egg
1 teaspoon vanilla extract

Thin and crisp, these cookies make for surefire after-dinner winners. Toasting the pecans, a native American nut, heightens their rich, buttery flavor.

Preheat the oven to 350°F. Line baking sheets with parchment paper.

In a medium bowl, combine ½ cup of the pecans, the oats, brown sugar, and flour.

In a large bowl, combine the butter, egg, and vanilla extract. Add the pecan mixture and stir until well-combined.

Drop by teaspoonfuls about 2" apart onto the prepared baking sheets. Top each cookie with ¼ teaspoon pecans. Bake for 8 minutes, or until the edges are lightly browned. Cool on a rack for 2 minutes. Slide the parchment paper off the baking sheet. Peel off the cookies and place on the rack to cool completely.

Makes 36

Per cookie: 56 calories, 1 g protein, 9 g carbohydrates, 3 g fat, 8 mg cholesterol, 1 g fiber, 13 mg sodium

Peanut Butter Cookies

1   cup unbleached all-purpose flour

½   teaspoon baking soda

½   teaspoon salt

½   cup butter, at room temperature

¾   cup granulated sugar

¼   cup packed brown sugar

1   egg

1   cup creamy peanut butter

½   teaspoon vanilla extract

1   cup coarsely chopped dry roasted, unsalted peanuts

Peanut aficionados: Get double the pleasure with these simple-to-make cookies. They're packed with creamy peanut butter and chopped peanuts.

Preheat the oven to 375°F. Grease baking sheets.

In a medium bowl, combine the flour, baking soda, and salt.

In a large bowl, with an electric mixer on medium speed, beat the butter, granulated sugar, and brown sugar for 3 minutes, or until light and fluffy. Beat in the egg, peanut butter, and vanilla extract. Beat in the flour mixture, a little at a time, until well-blended. Stir in the nuts.

Shape the dough into 1" balls. Arrange on the prepared baking sheets. Press flat with a fork. Bake for 10 minutes, or just until cookies start to brown. Cool on a rack for 2 minutes. Remove to the rack to cool completely.

Makes 50

Per cookie: 84 calories, 3 g protein, 7 g carbohydrates, 6 g fat, 9 mg cholesterol, 1 g fiber, 44 mg sodium

Toasted Pecan Cookies on page 30; Peanut Butter Cookies on page 31

Thumbprint Cookies

2 cups rolled oats

1¾ cups unbleached all-purpose flour

1 teaspoon baking powder

½ teaspoon salt

¾ cup butter, at room temperature

1 cup packed brown sugar

1 egg

1 teaspoon vanilla extract

¼ cup black raspberry all-fruit spread

¼ cup apricot all-fruit spread

In these moist treats, a spoonful of your favorite jam—black raspberry or apricot—nestles in a delightful oat cookie base.

Preheat the oven to 350°F. Grease baking sheets.

In a medium bowl, combine the oats, flour, baking powder, and salt.

In a large bowl, with an electric mixer on medium speed, beat the butter and brown sugar for 3 minutes, or until light and fluffy. Beat in the egg and vanilla extract. Beat in the flour mixture, a little at a time, until well-blended.

Shape the mixture into 1" balls and place on the prepared baking sheets, leaving 2" between the cookies. Dip your thumb into water and make an indentation in the center of each cookie. Spoon ½ teaspoon of the raspberry spread into the centers of half of the cookies. Fill the remaining cookies with the apricot spread.

Bake for 12 minutes, or until lightly browned and firm to the touch.

Cool on a rack for 2 minutes. Remove to the rack to cool completely.

Makes 45

Per cookie: 97 calories, 2 g protein, 16 g carbohydrates, 4 g fat, 13 mg cholesterol, 1 g fiber, 65 mg sodium

Maple Cookies

2 cups unbleached all-purpose flour

½ cup ground walnuts

1 teaspoon cream of tartar

1 teaspoon baking soda

1 cup butter, at room temperature

1½ cups confectioners' sugar + additional for garnish

2 egg yolks

1½ teaspoons maple extract

The enchanting combination of maple and walnuts makes these buttery cookies stand out. Dusted with confectioners' sugar, they're charming enough for a holiday platter, yet simple enough for a weekday treat.

Preheat the oven to 325°F.

In a medium bowl, combine the flour, walnuts, cream of tartar, and baking soda.

In a large bowl, with an electric mixer on medium speed, beat the butter and 1½ cups confectioners' sugar for 3 minutes, or until light and fluffy. Beat in the egg yolks and maple extract. Beat in the flour mixture a little at a time until well-blended.

Shape into 2" balls. Arrange about 2" apart on ungreased baking sheets. Using the bottom of a glass, flatten each cookie slightly. Bake for 12 minutes, or until lightly browned. Cool on a rack for 2 minutes. Remove to the rack to cool completely. Sprinkle liberally with confectioners' sugar, if desired.

Makes 40

Per cookie: 114 calories, 2 g protein, 11 g carbohydrates, 8 g fat, 27 mg cholesterol, 1 g fiber, 91 mg sodium

Tofokies

1¾ cups
purpo

½ teasp

¼ teasp

1 cup b
temp

¾ cup g

½ cup p

1 egg

1 teasp

1 cup E

4 ounces semisweet
chocolate, melted

Then you're sure to adore these cookies, which *bits and semisweet chocolate.*

 to 375°F.

, combine the flour, baking soda, and salt.

ith an electric mixer on medium speed, anulated sugar, and brown sugar for 3 ght and fluffy. Beat in the egg and vanilla flour mixture, a little at a time, until well- toffee bits.

fuls about 2" apart onto ungreased baking sheets. Bake for minutes, or until light brown. Cool on a rack for 2 minutes. Remove to the rack to cool completely.

Dip half of each cookie into the chocolate. Let cool on a rack until hardened.

Makes 72

Per cookie: 75 calories, 1 g protein, 9 g carbohydrates, 5 g fat, 12 mg cholesterol, 1 g fiber, 55 mg sodium

Almond and Oat Bars on page 38

Gingersnaps

2 cups unbleached all-purpose flour

1 teaspoon baking soda

1 teaspoon ground cinnamon

1 tablespoon ground ginger

½ teaspoon salt

⅛ teaspoon freshly ground nutmeg

¾ cup butter, at room temperature

¾ cup packed brown sugar

1 egg

½ cup molasses

Confectioners' sugar (optional)

When only a crisp cookie with plenty of ginger punch will do, give this recipe a shot. It's sure to please.

Preheat the oven to 350°F.

In a medium bowl, combine the flour, baking soda, cinnamon, ginger, salt, and nutmeg.

In a large bowl, with an electric mixer on medium speed, beat the butter and brown sugar for 3 minutes, or until light and fluffy. Beat in the egg and molasses. Beat in the flour mixture, a little at a time, until well-blended.

Shape into ½" balls. Arrange about 2" apart on ungreased baking sheets. Bake for 10 minutes, or until tops are slightly rounded and lightly browned. Cool on a rack for 2 minutes. Remove to the rack to cool completely. Dust with the confectioners' sugar, if desired

Makes 64

Per cookie: 49 calories, 1 g protein, 7 g carbohydrates, 3 g fat, 10 mg cholesterol, 1 g fiber, 64 mg sodium

Almond and Oat Bars

These quick-to-make granola bars have all your favorites: semisweet chocolate, coconut, and slivered almonds.

1½ cups unbleached all-purpose flour

1½ cups rolled oats

½ teaspoon salt

1 cup butter, at room temperature

½ cup packed brown sugar

1 teaspoon vanilla extract

1 cup mini semisweet chocolate chips

½ cup flaked coconut

½ cup slivered almonds, coarsely chopped

Preheat the oven to 350°F.

In a medium bowl, combine the flour, oats, and salt.

In a large bowl, with an electric mixer on medium speed, beat the butter, brown sugar, and vanilla extract for 3 minutes, or until light and fluffy. Beat in the flour mixture, a little at a time, until well-blended. Stir in the chocolate chips, coconut, and almonds.

Spread in an ungreased 13" x 9" baking pan. Bake for 25 minutes, or until light brown. Cool completely on a rack. Cut into 40 bars.

Makes 40

Per bar: 149 calories, 3 g protein, 17 g carbohydrates, 9 g fat, 15 mg cholesterol, 1 g fiber, 90 mg sodium

Chocolate-Walnut Biscotti

1½ cups unbleached all-purpose flour

⅓ cup unsweetened cocoa powder

1½ teaspoons baking powder

1 teaspoon instant coffee powder

¼ teaspoon salt

6 tablespoons butter, at room temperature

¾ cup sugar

2 eggs

2 teaspoons vanilla extract

½ cup coarsely chopped walnuts

Twice-baked for incredible crunch, these Italian-style treats beg for dipping in coffee or cappuccino.

Preheat the oven to 350°F. Grease a baking sheet.

In a medium bowl, combine the flour, cocoa powder, baking powder, coffee powder, and salt.

In a large bowl, with an electric mixer on medium speed, beat the butter and sugar for 3 minutes, or until light and fluffy. Beat in the eggs and vanilla extract. Beat in the flour mixture, a little at a time, until well-blended. Stir in the walnuts.

Place the dough on the prepared baking sheet, shaping to form a log about 9" long and 5" wide.

Bake for 20 minutes, or until top springs back when lightly touched. Remove to a rack to cool for 10 minutes. Reduce the oven temperature to 300°F.

Cut the log, on a slight diagonal, into ½"-thick slices. Place, cut side down, on the baking sheet, and bake for 15 minutes. Turn the slices over and bake for 10 minutes longer, or until dry. Cool on a rack for 2 minutes. Remove to the rack to cool completely.

Makes 18

Per cookie: 172 calories, 4 g protein, 20 g carbohydrates, 9 g fat, 35 mg cholesterol, 1 g fiber, 118 mg sodium

Almond-Orange Biscotti

1¾ cups unbleached all-purpose flour

½ cup cornmeal

1½ teaspoons baking powder

¼ teaspoon salt

½ cup unsalted butter, at room temperature

¾ cup sugar

2 eggs

½ teaspoon orange extract

1 teaspoon grated orange peel

¾ cup whole, natural almonds, toasted and chopped

Classic biscotti flavorings include nuts and seeds. Here, almonds and orange peel get the nod. Enjoy with a cup of espresso or hot chocolate.

Preheat the oven to 350°F. Grease a baking sheet.

In a medium bowl, combine the flour, cornmeal, baking powder, and salt.

In a large bowl, with an electric mixer on medium speed, beat the butter and sugar for 3 minutes, or until light and fluffy. Beat in the eggs, orange extract, and orange peel. Beat in the flour mixture, a little at a time, until well-blended. Stir in the almonds. Divide the dough into 2 equal-size pieces. Refrigerate for 30 minutes, or until firm.

Shape each piece into a 12"-long log and place both on the prepared baking sheet. Bake for 45 minutes, or until golden. Remove to a rack to cool for 10 minutes. Reduce the oven temperature to 300°F.

Cut each log, on a slight diagonal, into 12 ½"-thick slices. Place, cut side down, on the baking sheet and bake for 15 minutes. Turn the slices over and bake for 10 minutes longer, or until dry. Cool on a rack for 2 minutes. Remove to the rack to cool completely.

Makes 24

Per cookie: 150 calories, 4 g protein, 16 g carbohydrates, 9 g fat, 29 mg cholesterol, 1 g fiber, 57 mg sodium

Almond Spritz Cookies on page 44

Orange Sugar Cutout Cookies

2¼ cups unbleached all-purpose flour
1 teaspoon baking powder
¼ teaspoon salt
¾ cup butter, at room temperature
¾ cup granulated sugar
2 eggs
2 tablespoons orange juice
1 teaspoon grated orange peel
½ teaspoon orange extract
1 egg white
2 tablespoons water
Colored sugar

Cut into fun shapes, then decorated with colored sugar, these crisp goodies will certainly charm their way onto any holiday cookie platter.

In a medium bowl, combine the flour, baking powder, and salt.

In a large bowl, with an electric mixer on medium speed, beat the butter and granulated sugar for 3 minutes, or until light and fluffy. Beat in the eggs, orange juice, orange peel, and orange extract. Beat in the flour mixture, a little at a time, until well-blended.

Divide the dough into thirds, wrap each portion in plastic wrap, and refrigerate for 3 hours.

Preheat the oven to 350°F. Grease baking sheets. Mix the egg white with the water.

Place one-third of the dough on a lightly floured surface, leaving the remaining two-thirds in the refrigerator. Using a floured rolling pin, roll to ⅛" thickness. Using floured cookie cutters, cut into shapes. Arrange on the prepared baking sheets. Lightly brush each cookie with the egg white mixture. Sprinkle with the colored sugar. Repeat until all the dough has been used.

Bake for 11 minutes, or until lightly browned. Cool on a rack for 2 minutes. Remove to the rack to cool completely.

Makes 80
Per cookie: 40 calories, 1 g protein, 5 g carbohydrates, 3 g fat, 13 mg cholesterol, 1 g fiber, 34 mg sodium

Almond Spritz Cookies

2½ cups unbleached all-purpose flour

½ teaspoon salt

1 cup butter, at room temperature

1 package (3 ounces) cream cheese, at room temperature

1 cup granulated sugar

1 egg yolk

1 teaspoon almond extract

Colored sugar (optional)

Cream cheese, in addition to the usual butter, gives these versatile pressed cookies superb texture and flavor. Serve them plain or decorated, or turn them into chocolate-filled cookie sandwiches.

Preheat the oven to 350°F. Grease baking sheets.

In a medium bowl, combine the flour and salt.

In a large bowl, with an electric mixer on medium speed, beat the butter, cream cheese, and granulated sugar for 3 minutes, or until light and fluffy. Beat in the egg yolk and almond extract. Beat in the flour mixture, a little at a time, until well-blended.

Place the dough in a cookie press and form a variety of shapes. Sprinkle with colored sugar (if using). Bake for 11 minutes, or until the edges are lightly browned. Cool on a rack for 2 minutes. Remove to the rack to cool completely.

Makes 80

Per cookie: 76 calories, 2 g protein, 10 g carbohydrates, 4 g fat, 12 mg cholesterol, 1 g fiber, 57 mg sodium

---

COOKING TIP

To make cookie sandwiches, melt 1 cup chocolate chips. Using a spatula, spread the chocolate between two cookies and press together lightly. Place on a rack until set.

Rich Butter Sandwich Cookies

2½ cups unbleached all-purpose flour
1 teaspoon baking powder
½ teaspoon salt
1 cup butter, at room temperature
1 cup sugar
2 eggs
1 tablespoon vanilla extract
4 ounces bittersweet chocolate, melted

Tasters agree: These are the best-ever cookies in their class. They're light. They're tender. They're buttery. And they're fuss-free to make, too.

In a medium bowl, combine the flour, baking powder, and salt.

In a large bowl, with an electric mixer on medium speed, beat the butter and sugar for 3 minutes, or until light and fluffy. Beat in the eggs and vanilla extract. Beat in the flour mixture, a little at a time, until well-blended.

Divide the dough in half. Place each half on a large piece of plastic wrap. Roll and shape each half into an 8" x 2" log. Wrap and freeze for 30 minutes, or until firm.

Preheat the oven to 375°F. Cut each log into ¼"-thick slices. Arrange 2" apart on ungreased baking sheets. Bake for 8 minutes, or until golden brown. Cool on a rack for 2 minutes. Remove to the rack to cool completely.

To make butter sandwich cookies, spread the melted chocolate on half the cookies. Top with the remaining half.

Makes 25
Per cookie: 187 calories, 3 g protein, 23 g carbohydrates, 11 g fat, 39 mg cholesterol, 1 g fiber, 148 mg sodium

Gingerbread Cookies

2½   **cups unbleached all-purpose flour**

1   **tablespoon ground cinnamon**

2   **teaspoons ground ginger**

1   **teaspoon baking soda**

¼   **teaspoon ground nutmeg**

¼   **teaspoon ground cloves**

¼   **teaspoon salt**

6   **tablespoons butter, at room temperature**

¾   **cup packed brown sugar**

2   **tablespoons molasses**

¼–⅓   **cup water**

    Royal Icing (see recipe, page 48)

Wow family and guests with these adorable—and tasty—ginger and spice boys and girls. Perfect for taking to a neighborhood cookie exchange or serving to Santa with a glass of milk.

Preheat the oven to 375°F. Grease baking sheets.

In a medium bowl, combine the flour, cinnamon, ginger, baking soda, nutmeg, cloves, and salt.

In a large bowl, with an electric mixer on medium speed, beat the butter and brown sugar for 3 minutes, or until light and fluffy. Beat in the molasses. Beat in the flour mixture, a little at a time, until well-blended. Add the water, 1 tablespoon at a time, to form a stiff but well-blended dough.

Divide the dough into four equal-sized pieces. Roll each piece out to ¼" thickness. Using cookie cutters, cut into shapes. Arrange on the prepared baking sheets, leaving 1" between the cookies.

Bake for 7 minutes, or until lightly browned. Cool on a rack for 2 minutes. Remove to the rack to cool completely.

When completely cooled, decorate with the icing.

Makes 40

Per cookie: 96 calories, 2 g protein, 19 g carbohydrates, 3 g fat, 6 mg cholesterol, 1 g fiber, 60 mg sodium

Royal Icing

2   **teaspoons powdered egg whites**

2   **tablespoons water**

2   **cups confectioners' sugar**

1   **teaspoon vanilla extract**

Pipe or drizzle this extra-easy icing onto cookies for a decorative appearance.

In a large bowl, with an electric mixer on high speed, beat the powdered egg whites and water until well-blended. Gradually add the confectioners' sugar and vanilla extract, beating constantly. Add more water, a teaspoon at a time, as necessary to make a smooth icing. (Add still more if the icing starts to thicken while decorating.)

Drizzle or pipe over cookies.

COOKING TIP

The best way to color the icing is to add food color paste to the finished icing. Remove a small bit of icing to a bowl and use a wooden pick to stir in a tiny bit of paste. Add more paste or icing to reach desired color. Cover with plastic wrap until ready to use. Repeat with remaining icing and colors.

Food color paste is available in cooking stores, craft stores, some supermarkets, or where cake decorating products are available.

BEST-EVER
BROWNIES

Rich Glazed Brownies

4   squares (1 ounce each) unsweetened chocolate

½   cup butter

2   cups sugar

4   eggs

1   tablespoon vanilla extract

1   cup unbleached all-purpose flour

¾   cup bittersweet or double-chocolate chocolate chips

Looking for a decadent chocolate dessert? Search no more. These luxurious fudgy brownies, topped with a silky bittersweet glaze, will satisfy your quest.

Preheat the oven to 375°F. Grease a 13" x 9" baking pan.

Place the chocolate and butter in a microwaveable bowl. Microwave on high for 4 minutes, or until the butter is melted.

Remove from the microwave oven and stir constantly to fully melt the chocolate. Stir in the sugar until well-blended. Add the eggs, one at a time, stirring after each addition, until well-blended. Stir in the vanilla extract and flour.

Spread into the prepared pan. Bake for 40 minutes, or until a wooden pick inserted in the center comes out clean. Place on a rack and cool slightly. Place the chips on the warm brownies and spread to form a glaze. Cool in the pan on a rack.

Makes 32

Per brownie: 137 calories, 2 g protein, 19 g carbohydrates, 7 g fat, 35 mg cholesterol, 1 g fiber, 40 mg sodium

Walnut Brownies

1 cup unbleached all-purpose flour

6 tablespoons unsweetened cocoa powder

½ teaspoon baking powder

¼ teaspoon salt

½ cup unsalted butter, melted

1 cup sugar

2 eggs

2 teaspoons vanilla extract

½ cup coarsely chopped walnuts

Unadorned except for one of America's favorite baking nuts, these brownies make for a divine everyday treat.

Preheat the oven to 350°F. Grease an 8" x 8" baking pan.

In a medium bowl, combine the flour, cocoa powder, baking powder, and salt.

In a large bowl, stir together the butter and sugar until well-blended. Beat in the eggs and vanilla extract. Add the flour mixture and stir until just well-blended. Stir in the walnuts.

Spread into the prepared pan. Bake for 30 minutes, or until a wooden pick inserted in the center comes out clean. Cool in the pan on a rack.

Makes 16

Per brownie: 208 calories, 6 g protein, 22 g carbohydrates, 12 g fat, 43 mg cholesterol, 1 g fiber, 63 mg sodium

Rocky Road Brownies

4 squares (1 ounce each) unsweetened chocolate

½ cup butter

2 cups packed brown sugar

4 eggs

1 tablespoon vanilla extract

1 cup unbleached all-purpose flour

1 cup miniature marshmallows

1 cup semisweet chocolate chunks

½ cup pecan halves, broken into pieces

The classic combination of chocolate, marshmallows, and nuts is delicious packed into rich, thick brownies.

Preheat the oven to 375°F. Grease a 13" x 9" baking pan.

Place the chocolate and butter in a microwaveable bowl. Microwave on high for 2 minutes, or until the butter is melted.

Remove from microwave oven and stir constantly to fully melt the chocolate. Stir in the brown sugar until well-blended. Add the eggs, one at a time, stirring after each addition, until well-blended. Stir in the vanilla extract and flour. Stir in half of the marshmallows, half of the chocolate chunks, and half of the pecans.

Spread into the prepared pan. Sprinkle the remaining marshmallows, chocolate chunks, and pecans over the brownies. Bake for 40 minutes, or until a wooden pick inserted in the center comes out clean. Cool in the pan on a rack.

Makes 32

Per brownie: 149 calories, 3 g protein, 19 g carbohydrates, 8 g fat, 35 mg cholesterol, 1 g fiber, 46 mg sodium

Double Espresso Brownies

Brownies

¾ cup unbleached all-purpose flour

2 teaspoons instant espresso powder

½ teaspoon baking powder

¼ teaspoon salt

2 squares (1 ounce each) unsweetened chocolate

⅓ cup unsalted butter

1 cup granulated sugar

2 eggs

½ teaspoon vanilla extract

Frosting

½ cup semisweet chocolate chips

2 tablespoons butter

1 teaspoon instant espresso powder

2 tablespoons half-and-half

½ cup confectioners' sugar

Get the devilish java kick twice—once in the fudgelike brownies and once in the creamy frosting. No espresso on hand? You could substitute everyday instant coffee powder.

To make the brownies: Preheat the oven to 350°F. Grease an 8" x 8" baking pan.

In a medium bowl, combine the flour, espresso powder, baking powder, and salt. Place the chocolate and butter in a microwaveable bowl. Microwave on high for 4 minutes, or until the butter is melted.

Remove from the microwave oven, stirring constantly to fully melt the chocolate. Stir in the granulated sugar until well-blended. Add the eggs, one at a time, stirring after each addition, until well-blended. Stir in the vanilla extract and the flour mixture.

Spread into the prepared pan. Bake for 30 minutes, or until a wooden pick inserted in the center comes out clean. Cool in the pan on a rack.

To make the frosting: In a small saucepan, combine the chocolate chips, butter, espresso powder, and half-and-half. Heat, stirring constantly, until smooth. Stir in the confectioners' sugar until smooth. Spread over the brownies. Let the frosting cool.

Makes 16

Per brownie: 188 calories, 3 g protein, 25 g carbohydrates, 11 g fat, 43 mg cholesterol, 1 g fiber, 75 mg sodium

Brownie Pie

¾ cup unbleached all-
  purpose flour
½ cup ground walnuts
½ teaspoon baking powder
¼ teaspoon salt
2 squares (1 ounce each)
  unsweetened chocolate
½ cup butter
1 cup granulated sugar
2 eggs
1½ teaspoons vanilla extract
12 walnut halves
  Confectioners' sugar

The shape is unusual, but the taste is familiar—deep, rich chocolate with walnuts. Serve a wedge with a scoop of vanilla-fudge ice cream for a special dessert treat.

Preheat the oven to 350°F. Grease a 9"-round tart pan with removable bottom.

In a medium bowl, combine the flour, ground walnuts, baking powder, and salt.

Place the chocolate and butter in a microwaveable bowl. Microwave on high for 4 minutes, or until the butter is melted.

Remove from the microwave oven, stirring constantly to fully melt the chocolate. Stir in the granulated sugar. Add the eggs, one at a time, stirring after each addition, until well-blended. Stir in the vanilla extract and the flour mixture.

Spread into the prepared pan. Bake for 25 minutes, or until a wooden pick inserted in the center comes out clean. Cool in the pan on a rack for 10 minutes. Remove from the pan. Arrange the walnut halves on the top. Dust with the confectioners' sugar.

Makes 12
Per brownie: 244 calories, 5 g protein, 19 g carbohydrates, 18 g fat, 58 mg cholesterol, 2 g fiber, 160 mg sodium

Cherry Brownies

Brownies

1 cup unbleached all-purpose flour
¾ teaspoon baking powder
½ teaspoon salt
4 squares (1 ounce each) unsweetened chocolate
⅔ cup butter
2 cups granulated sugar
4 eggs
1½ teaspoons vanilla extract
1 cup cherry all-fruit spread

Frosting

4 tablespoons butter, at room temperature
4 teaspoons half-and-half
½ teaspoon almond extract
1½ cups confectioners' sugar

After tasting these superb moist brownies, you're sure to be forever hooked on the chocolate-cherry connection. An almond-flavored frosting tops the treat.

To make the brownies: Preheat the oven to 350°F. Grease a 13" x 9" baking pan.

In a medium bowl, combine the flour, baking powder, and salt.

Place the chocolate and butter in a microwaveable bowl. Microwave on high for 4 minutes, or until the butter is melted.

Remove from the microwave oven, stirring constantly to fully melt the chocolate. Stir in the granulated sugar. Add the eggs, one at a time, stirring after each addition, until well-blended. Stir in the vanilla extract and the flour mixture.

Spread into the prepared pan. Using a knife, swirl in the cherry spread. Bake for 35 minutes, or until a wooden pick inserted in the center comes out clean. Cool in the pan on a rack.

To make the frosting: Combine the butter, half-and-half, almond extract, and confectioners' sugar in a small bowl. Beat until smooth and creamy. Spread over the brownies.

Makes 32

Per brownie: 194 calories, 2 g protein, 28 g carbohydrates, 9 g fat, 42 mg cholesterol, 1 g fiber, 116 mg sodium

Marbled Brownies

5 squares (1 ounce each) unsweetened chocolate

¾ cup butter

1¾ cups sugar

3 eggs

1 tablespoon vanilla extract

1 cup + 1 tablespoon unbleached all-purpose flour

8 ounces cream cheese, at room temperature

1 egg yolk

Cheesecake filling is swirled through these brownies creating a rich, delicate flavor.

Preheat the oven to 375°F. Grease an 8" x 8" baking pan.

Place the chocolate and butter in a microwaveable bowl. Microwave on high for 4 minutes, or until the butter is melted.

Remove from the microwave oven, stirring constantly to fully melt the chocolate. Stir in 1½ cups sugar until well-blended. Add the 3 whole eggs, one at a time, stirring after each addition, until well-blended. Stir in the vanilla extract and 1 cup of the flour.

Spread into the prepared pan.

In a small bowl, with an electric mixer on low speed, beat the cream cheese, egg yolk, the remaining ¼ cup sugar, and the remaining 1 tablespoon flour until creamy, about 3 minutes. Pour on top of the brownies and, using a knife, swirl to marble. Bake for 40 minutes, or until a wooden pick inserted in the center comes out clean. Place on a rack and cool slightly. Cool in the pan on the rack.

Makes 32

Per brownie: 148 calories, 3 g protein, 16 g carbohydrates, 10 g fat, 44 mg cholesterol, 1 g fiber, 84 mg sodium

Low-Fat Fudgy Brownies

½ cup unbleached all-purpose flour

¾ cup unsweetened cocoa powder

½ teaspoon baking powder

¼ teaspoon salt

3 egg whites

2 eggs, lightly beaten

1 cup granulated sugar

½ cup packed brown sugar

⅔ cup unsweetened applesauce

2 teaspoons vanilla extract

½ cup coarsely chopped walnuts

Confectioners' sugar

Splurge on these brownies often and without guilt. They're tender, moist, chocolatey, and, thanks to the applesauce which replaces the usual butter, nicely low in fat.

Preheat the oven to 350°F. Grease a 13" x 9" baking pan.

In a medium bowl, combine the flour, cocoa powder, baking powder, and salt.

In a large bowl, with an electric mixer on low speed, beat the egg whites until foamy. Gently stir in the eggs, granulated sugar, and brown sugar until well-combined. Blend in the applesauce and vanilla extract. Stir in the flour mixture. Stir in the walnuts.

Spread into the prepared pan. Bake for 30 minutes, or until a wooden pick inserted in the center comes out clean. Do not over bake. Cool in the pan on a rack. Dust the confectioners' sugar over the brownies.

Makes 32

Per brownie: 90 calories, 4 g protein, 14 g carbohydrates, 4 g fat, 14 mg cholesterol, 1 g fiber, 38 mg sodium

Raspberry-Laced Brownies

1⅔ cups confectioners' sugar

⅔ cup cake flour

¼ cup unsweetened cocoa powder

¾ teaspoon baking powder

⅛ teaspoon salt

1½ squares (1 ounce each) unsweetened chocolate

2½ tablespoons vegetable oil

2 tablespoons dark corn syrup

2 teaspoons vanilla extract

2 egg whites

2 tablespoons raspberry jam

½ cup raspberries

Here's a combination—raspberry and chocolate—that's made in heaven. Enjoy these lower-fat bites plain, with a dollop of whipped cream, or with a generous dip of vanilla frozen yogurt.

Preheat the oven to 350°F. Line a 9" x 9" baking pan with foil, wrapping the excess over the sides to form handles. Grease the foil.

In a medium bowl, combine the confectioners' sugar, flour, cocoa powder, baking powder, and salt.

In a large microwaveable bowl, combine the chocolate and oil. Microwave on high for 1 minute. Stir until smooth. Stir in the corn syrup, vanilla extract, and egg whites. Mix well. Gently stir in the flour mixture until just blended.

In a small microwaveable bowl, microwave the jam on high for 30 seconds, or until melted. Stir in the raspberries. Carefully fold into the batter, keeping most of the berries whole.

Spread into the prepared pan. Bake for 20 minutes, or until a wooden pick inserted in the center comes out clean. Let cool in the pan on a rack for 15 minutes. Using the overhanging foil as handles, lift the brownies from the pan. Let cool completely on the rack. Cut into bars, wiping the knife blade between cuts.

Makes 16

Per brownie: 109 calories, 2 g protein, 18 g carbohydrates, 5 g fat, 0 mg cholesterol, 1 g fiber, 54 mg sodium

Caramel-Glazed Brownies

1¼ cups unbleached all-purpose flour

¼ teaspoon baking soda

¼ teaspoon salt

1½ cups sugar

⅓ cup butter

¼ cup 1% buttermilk

¾ cup Dutch processed or European-style cocoa powder

2 eggs

2 teaspoons vanilla extract

⅓ cup finely chopped, toasted almonds

¼ cup caramel topping

Here, caramel, a simple mixture of caramelized (browned) sugar, butter, and milk, atop cocoa-enhanced brownies makes for a sensuous dessert. The caramel is store-bought so the whole treat is a breeze to make.

Preheat the oven to 350°F. Grease a 13" x 9" baking dish with cooking spray.

In a medium bowl, combine the flour, baking soda, and salt.

In a large saucepan, combine the sugar, butter, and buttermilk. Bring just to a boil over medium heat, stirring constantly. Remove from the heat. Stir in the cocoa powder until smooth. Stir in the eggs, one at a time. Stir in the vanilla extract. Mix in the flour mixture. Stir in the almonds.

Spread into the prepared baking pan. Bake for 18 minutes, or until a wooden pick inserted in the center comes out clean. Drizzle the caramel topping over the brownies. Cool in the pan on a rack.

Makes 32
Per brownie: 98 calories, 3 g protein, 14 g carbohydrates, 4 g fat, 20 mg cholesterol, 1 g fiber, 57 mg sodium

Brownie Cake Squares

⅔ cup unbleached all-purpose flour

⅔ cup granulated sugar

⅓ cup unsweetened cocoa powder

1 teaspoon baking powder

¼ teaspoon salt

⅔ cup fat-free evaporated milk

⅓ cup butter, melted

1 egg

1½ teaspoons vanilla extract

Confectioners' sugar

When only a cakelike brownie will do, give these squares a whirl. They're light. They're tender. They're just what your tastebuds crave.

Preheat the oven to 350°F. Grease an 8" x 8" baking pan.

In a medium bowl, combine the flour, granulated sugar, cocoa powder, baking powder, and salt.

In another bowl, combine the milk, butter, egg, and vanilla extract. Stir in the flour mixture.

Spread into the prepared pan. Bake for 30 minutes, or until a wooden pick inserted in the center comes out clean. Cool in the pan on a rack. Dust with the confectioners' sugar.

Makes 16

Per brownie: 112 calories, 4 g protein, 14 g carbohydrates, 5 g fat, 25 mg cholesterol, 0 g fiber, 121 mg sodium

Iced Butterscotch Brownies

1   cup unbleached all-purpose flour

½   teaspoon baking powder

¼   teaspoon salt

⅓   cup butter

½   cup packed brown sugar

2   eggs

2   teaspoons vanilla extract

¾   cup butterscotch-flavored chips

Brown sugar and butter combine for the delectable flavor known as butterscotch. In this recipe, butterscotch chips ice the butterscotch bars for double the enjoyment.

Preheat the oven to 350°F. Grease an 8" x 8" baking pan.

In a medium bowl, combine the flour, baking powder, and salt.

In a large bowl, with an electric mixer on medium speed, beat the butter and brown sugar until creamy, about 3 minutes. Beat in the eggs and vanilla extract. Add the flour mixture and beat until just blended.

Spread into the prepared pan. Bake for 30 minutes, or until a wooden pick inserted in the center comes out clean. Place on a rack. Place the chips on the warm brownies and spread with a spatula to ice. Cool in the pan on a rack.

Makes 16

Per brownie: 142 calories, 3 g protein, 19 g carbohydrates, 8 g fat, 38 mg cholesterol, 1 g fiber, 102 mg sodium

Coconut Blondies

1¼ cups unbleached all-purpose flour

½ teaspoon baking powder

¼ teaspoon salt

½ cup butter, at room temperature

¾ cup packed light brown sugar

2 eggs

1 teaspoon vanilla extract

½ cup flaked coconut

There's nothing dull about these vanilla "brownies." Coconut enlivens the basic recipe.

Preheat the oven to 350°F. Grease an 8" x 8" baking pan.

In a medium bowl, combine the flour, baking powder, and salt.

In a large bowl, with an electric mixer on medium speed, beat the butter and brown sugar for 3 minutes, or until creamy. Beat in the eggs and vanilla extract. Add the flour mixture and beat until just blended. Stir in the coconut.

Spread into the prepared pan. Bake for 30 minutes, or until a wooden pick inserted in the center comes out clean. Cool in the pan on a rack.

Makes 36

Per blondie: 67 calories, 1 g protein, 9 g carbohydrates, 4 g fat, 20 mg cholesterol, 1 g fiber, 55 mg sodium

Fruit-Studded Blondies

Blondies

1½ cups unbleached all-purpose flour

1 teaspoon baking powder

¼ teaspoon salt

½ cup butter, at room temperature

¾ cup packed brown sugar

2 eggs

2 teaspoons vanilla extract

1 cup chopped dates

1 cup dried cranberries

½ teaspoon grated orange peel

Glaze

6 tablespoons butter

¼ cup packed brown sugar

1½ tablespoons dark corn syrup

Be different. Lace butterscotch brownies with cranberries and dates, and top them with a simply great-tasting caramel glaze. Result: blondies, like these, worthy of company, but easy enough for every day.

To make the blondies: Preheat the oven to 350°F. Grease a 13" x 9" baking pan.

In a medium bowl, combine the flour, baking powder, and salt.

In a large bowl, with an electric mixer on medium speed, beat the butter and brown sugar for 3 minutes, or until creamy. Beat in the eggs and vanilla extract. Add the flour mixture and beat until just blended. Stir in the dates, cranberries, and orange peel.

Spread into the prepared pan. Bake for 20 minutes, or until a wooden pick inserted in the center comes out clean. Cool in the pan on a rack.

To make the glaze: Combine the butter, brown sugar, and corn syrup in a small saucepan. Bring to a boil over medium heat, stirring frequently. Simmer for 3 minutes without stirring. Spread over the blondies. Cool in the pan on a rack.

Makes 36

Per blondie: 130 calories, 2 g protein, 21 g carbohydrates, 6 g fat, 25 mg cholesterol, 1 g fiber, 82 mg sodium

SWEET AND SIMPLE MUFFINS

Blueberry Muffins

1¾ cups unbleached all-purpose flour

2 teaspoons baking powder

½ teaspoon salt

½ teaspoon cinnamon

½ cup milk

¼ cup vegetable oil

1 egg

½ cup sugar

1 teaspoon vanilla extract

1½ cups blueberries

These classic muffins are light with a golden brown crust and a slightly sweet flavor—everything great muffins should be. For the best flavor and texture, enjoy these muffins the same day you make them.

Preheat the oven to 400°F. Grease a 12-cup muffin pan.

In a medium bowl, combine the flour, baking powder, salt, and cinnamon.

In a large bowl, stir together the milk, oil, egg, sugar, and vanilla extract until well-blended. Stir in the flour mixture until just combined. Do not overmix. Gently fold in the blueberries.

Divide the batter evenly among the prepared muffin cups, filling them about two-thirds full. Bake for 17 to 20 minutes, or until a wooden pick inserted in the center of a muffin comes out clean. Cool on a rack for 5 minutes. Remove to the rack to cool completely.

Makes 12

Per muffin: 126 calories, 2 g protein, 18 g carbohydrates, 6 g fat, 20 mg cholesterol, 1 g fiber, 176 mg sodium

Chocolate-Raspberry Muffins

This is a lovely combination of raspberries bathed in chocolate.

1½ cups unbleached all-purpose flour

¼ cup unsweetened cocoa powder

1½ teaspoons baking powder

1 teaspoon ground cinnamon

½ teaspoon baking soda

½ teaspoon salt

¾ cup buttermilk

¼ cup vegetable oil

1 egg

1 cup raspberries

Preheat the oven to 400°F. Grease a 12-cup muffin pan.

In a medium bowl, combine the flour, cocoa powder, baking powder, cinnamon, baking soda, and salt.

In a large bowl, stir together the buttermilk, oil, and egg until well-blended. Stir in the flour mixture until just combined. Do not overmix. Gently fold in the raspberries.

Divide the batter evenly among the prepared muffin cups, filling them about two-thirds full. Bake for 12 to 15 minutes, or until a wooden pick inserted in the center of a muffin comes out clean. Cool on a rack for 5 minutes. Remove to the rack to cool completely.

Makes 12

Per muffin: 151 calories, 5 g protein, 20 g carbohydrates, 7 g fat, 20 mg cholesterol, 1 g fiber, 164 mg sodium

Mint Chocolate Chip Muffins

1½ cups unbleached all-purpose flour

¼ cup unsweetened cocoa powder

1½ teaspoons baking powder

½ teaspoon baking soda

¼ teaspoon salt

¾ cup buttermilk

¼ cup vegetable oil

½ cup packed brown sugar

1 egg

½ cup mint chocolate chips

Muffins aren't just for breakfast anymore. These mint chocolate chip goodies make for ideal nibbling after meals, between meals, or anytime a chocolate craving hits.

Preheat the oven to 400°F. Grease a 12-cup muffin pan.

In a medium bowl, combine the flour, cocoa powder, baking powder, baking soda, and salt.

In a large bowl, stir together the buttermilk, oil, brown sugar, and egg until well-blended. Stir in the flour mixture until just combined. Do not overmix. Fold in the chips.

Divide the batter evenly among the prepared muffin cups, filling them about two-thirds full. Bake for 12 to 15 minutes, or until a wooden pick inserted in the center of a muffin comes out clean. Cool on a rack for 5 minutes. Remove to the rack to cool completely.

Makes 12

Per muffin: 199 calories, 5 g protein, 27 g carbohydrates, 9 g fat, 20 mg cholesterol, 1 g fiber, 187 mg sodium

Sweet-Tart Cranberry Muffins

1½ cups unbleached all-purpose flour

2 teaspoons baking powder

½ teaspoon baking soda

¼ teaspoon salt

1 teaspoon grated orange peel

½ cup coarsely chopped fresh or frozen cranberries

½ cup coarsely chopped pitted dates

½ cup buttermilk

2 eggs

⅓ cup maple syrup

¼ cup vegetable oil

It's love at first bite when you sample these muffins. Dates provide sweetness; cranberries, the tartness.

Preheat the oven to 400°F. Grease a 12-cup muffin pan.

In a medium bowl, combine the flour, baking powder, baking soda, and salt. Add the orange peel, cranberries, and dates. Toss gently.

In a large bowl, stir together the buttermilk, eggs, maple syrup, and oil until well-blended. Stir in the flour mixture until just combined. Do not overmix.

Divide the batter evenly among the prepared muffin cups, filling them about two-thirds full. Bake for 12 to 15 minutes, or until a wooden pick inserted in the center of a muffin comes out clean. Cool on a rack for 5 minutes. Remove to the rack to cool completely.

Makes 12

Per muffin: 164 calories, 4 g protein, 26 g carbohydrates, 6 g fat, 36 mg cholesterol, 1 g fiber, 190 mg sodium

Apple-Walnut Muffins

1½ cups unbleached all-purpose flour

2 teaspoons baking powder

1 teaspoon baking soda

½ teaspoon ground cinnamon

¼ teaspoon salt

½ cup buttermilk

3 tablespoons vegetable oil

¼ cup packed brown sugar

1 egg

½ cup finely chopped, peeled apples

½ cup golden raisins (optional)

Chopped fresh apples, not the usual applesauce, flavor these moist muffins. Enjoy for breakfast or as a snack.

Preheat the oven to 400°F. Grease a 12-cup muffin pan.

In a medium bowl, combine the flour, baking powder, baking soda, cinnamon, and salt.

In a large bowl, stir together the buttermilk, oil, brown sugar, and egg. Stir in the flour mixture until just combined. Do not overmix. Stir in the apples and raisins (if using).

Divide the batter evenly among the prepared muffin cups, filling them about two-thirds full. Bake for 12 to 15 minutes, or until a wooden pick inserted in the center of a muffin comes out clean. Cool on a rack for 5 minutes. Remove to the rack to cool completely.

Makes 12

Per muffin: 198 calories, 4 g protein, 30 g carbohydrates, 8 g fat, 21 mg cholesterol, 1 g fiber, 252 mg sodium

Pumpkin Muffins

2   cups unbleached all-purpose flour

2   teaspoons baking powder

1½ teaspoons pumpkin pie spice

¼   teaspoon baking soda

½   teaspoon salt

½   cup butter, at room temperature

¾   cup sugar

2   eggs

1   cup canned solid-packed pumpkin

¼   cup milk

¼   cup dried cranberries

Here's a fall treat that's a breeze to stir together. Canned pumpkin lets you make and savor these year round.

Preheat the oven to 400°F. Grease a 12-cup muffin pan.

In a medium bowl, combine the flour, baking powder, pumpkin pie spice, baking soda, and salt.

In a large bowl, with an electric mixer on medium speed, beat the butter and sugar for 3 minutes, or until light and fluffy. Beat in the eggs, pumpkin, and milk. Stir in the flour mixture until just combined. Do not overmix. Stir in the cranberries.

Divide the batter evenly among the prepared muffin cups, filling them about two-thirds full. Bake for 12 to 15 minutes, or until a wooden pick inserted in the center of a muffin comes out clean. Cool on a rack for 5 minutes. Remove to the rack to cool completely.

Makes 12

Per muffin: 232 calories, 5 g protein, 34 g carbohydrates, 10 g fat, 58 mg cholesterol, 1 g fiber, 286 mg sodium

Pineapple Muffins

1   can (8 ounces) crushed pineapple, packed in juice

1¾   cups unbleached all-purpose flour

2   teaspoons baking powder

½   teaspoon baking soda

½   teaspoon ground cinnamon

¼   teaspoon salt

½   cup slivered almonds, toasted

¾   cup milk

3   tablespoons vegetable oil

1   egg

⅓   cup packed brown sugar

¼   cup shredded coconut

Pineapple and coconut jazz up these muffins. They're marvelously moist and scrumptiously sweet.

Preheat the oven to 400°F. Grease a 12-cup muffin pan.

Place the pineapple in a sieve over a 1-cup measure and press with the back of a spoon to remove the excess juice. Reserve the pineapple and ¼ cup of the juice.

In a medium bowl, combine the flour, baking powder, baking soda, cinnamon, salt, and almonds.

In a large bowl, stir together the milk, oil, egg, brown sugar, and reserved pineapple juice until well-blended. Stir in the pineapple. Stir in the flour mixture until just blended. Do not overmix.

Divide the batter evenly among the prepared muffin cups, filling them about two-thirds full. Sprinkle the coconut over the muffin batter. Bake for 12 to 15 minutes, or until the muffins are lightly browned and a wooden pick inserted in the center of a muffin comes out clean. Cool on a rack for 5 minutes. Remove to the rack to cool completely.

Makes 12

Per muffin: 217 calories, 6 g protein, 28 g carbohydrates, 10 g fat, 20 mg cholesterol, 2 g fiber, 185 mg sodium

Apricot-Pecan Muffins

1½ cups unbleached all-purpose flour
2 teaspoons baking powder
¼ teaspoon salt
¼ teaspoon ground nutmeg
¾ cup chopped dried apricots
¼ cup chopped pecans
¾ cup buttermilk
¼ cup vegetable oil
1 egg
¾ cup packed brown sugar

Like raisins, dates, and other dried fruits, apricots pack tons of concentrated flavor and sweetness into muffins. If apricots aren't a favorite, swap them, in this recipe, with equally delightful dried peaches or cherries.

Preheat the oven to 400°F. Grease a 12-cup muffin pan.

In a medium bowl, combine the flour, baking powder, salt, and nutmeg. Stir in the apricots and pecans.

In a large bowl, stir together the buttermilk, oil, egg, and brown sugar until well-blended. Stir in the flour mixture until just combined. Do not overmix.

Divide the batter evenly among the muffin cups, filling them about two-thirds full. Bake for 13 to 15 minutes, or until a wooden pick inserted in the center of a muffin comes out clean. Cool on a rack for 5 minutes. Remove to the rack to cool completely.

Makes 12

Per muffin: 193 calories, 4 g protein, 31 g carbohydrates, 7 g fat, 19 mg cholesterol, 1 g fiber, 143 mg sodium

Banana-Walnut Muffins

Topping

2   **tablespoons unbleached all-purpose flour**

2   **tablespoons ground walnuts**

2   **tablespoons sugar**

1   **tablespoon cold butter, cut into small pieces**

Muffins

2   **cups unbleached all-purpose flour**

2¼   **teaspoons baking powder**

¼   **teaspoon salt**

½   **cup coarsely chopped walnuts**

1   **large ripe banana, mashed (about ½ cup)**

⅓   **cup vegetable oil**

1   **egg**

½   **cup sugar**

1   **teaspoon grated orange peel**

¼–½ **cup milk**

Wondering what to do with an overripe banana? Ponder no more. Instead, whip up a batch of these smashingly delicious muffins. It's the smart—and tasty—thing to do.

To make the topping: In a small bowl, combine the flour, walnuts, and sugar. Using a pastry blender or 2 knives, cut in the butter until the mixture resembles coarse crumbs.

To make the muffins: Preheat the oven to 425°F. Grease a 12-cup muffin pan.

In a large bowl, combine the flour, baking powder, salt, and walnuts.

In a food processor, combine the banana, oil, egg, sugar, and orange peel. Process for 30 seconds, or until well-combined. Transfer the mixture to a 2-cup measure. Stir in enough of the milk to make 1¾ cups. Pour into the flour mixture, stirring until just combined. Do not overmix.

Divide the batter evenly among the prepared muffin cups, filling them about two-thirds full. Sprinkle the topping over the muffin batter. Bake for 14 to 16 minutes, or until a wooden pick inserted in the center of a muffin comes out clean. Cool on a rack for 5 minutes. Remove to the rack to cool completely.

Makes 12

Per muffin: 242 calories, 5 g protein, 31 g carbohydrates, 12 g fat, 22 mg cholesterol, 1 g fiber, 135 mg sodium

Carrot Muffins

Muffins

2   cups unbleached all-purpose flour
⅔   cup granulated sugar
1½   teaspoons baking soda
½   teaspoon ground cinnamon
¼   teaspoon ground mace
⅛   teaspoon ground cloves
¼   teaspoon salt
½   cup golden raisins
1   cup buttermilk
¼   cup vegetable oil
1   egg
1   teaspoon vanilla extract
1¼   cups finely shredded carrots

Frosting

¾   cup confectioners' sugar
3   tablespoons cream cheese, at room temperature
½–1 teaspoon milk
½   teaspoon vanilla extract

Impress family and friends with these miniature carrot cakes. They're spiced just right with cinnamon and cloves and are topped with a super-simple cream cheese frosting.

To make the muffins: Preheat the oven to 375°F. Grease a 12-cup muffin pan.

In a medium bowl, combine the flour, granulated sugar, baking soda, cinnamon, mace, cloves, and salt. Add the raisins. Toss gently to coat.

In a large bowl, stir together the buttermilk, oil, egg, and vanilla extract until well-blended. Stir in the carrots. Stir in the flour mixture until just combined. Do not overmix.

Divide the batter evenly among the prepared muffin cups, filling them about two-thirds full. Bake for 18 to 20 minutes, or until a wooden pick inserted in the center of a muffin comes out clean. Cool on a rack for 5 minutes. Remove to the rack to cool completely.

To make the frosting: Stir together the confectioners' sugar, cream cheese, milk, and vanilla extract in a bowl until well-blended. Spread over the cooled muffins.

Makes 12

Per muffin: 194 calories, 4 g protein, 34 g carbohydrates, 6 g fat, 18 mg cholesterol, 1 g fiber, 199 mg sodium

Sweet-Tart Cranberry Muffins on page 75; Pineapple Muffins on page 79; Bran Muffins on page 86

Cardamom Muffins

1½ cups unbleached all-purpose flour

2 teaspoons baking powder

1 teaspoon baking soda

½ teaspoon ground cardamom

½ teaspoon salt

¾ cup buttermilk

¼ cup butter, melted and cooled slightly

1 egg

⅓ cup sugar

1 tablespoon grated orange peel

Enjoy these simple muffins topped with a spoonful of your favorite jam along with a glass of milk for a quick breakfast or snack.

Preheat the oven to 400°F. Grease a 12-cup muffin pan.

In a medium bowl, combine the flour, baking powder, baking soda, cardamom, and salt.

In a large bowl, stir together the buttermilk, butter, egg, sugar, and orange peel until well-blended. Stir in the flour mixture until just combined. Do not overmix.

Divide the batter evenly among the prepared muffin cups, filling them about two-thirds full. Bake for 12 to 15 minutes, or until a wooden pick inserted in the center of a muffin comes out clean. Cool on a rack for 5 minutes. Remove to the rack to cool completely.

Makes 12

Per muffin: 133 calories, 3 g protein, 19 g carbohydrates, 5 g fat, 30 mg cholesterol, 0 g fiber, 328 mg sodium

Bran Muffins

1½ cups bran cereal
½ cup milk
⅓ cup raisins
1 cup unbleached all-purpose flour
1½ teaspoons baking soda
½ teaspoon salt
1 egg
1 cup (8 ounces) sour cream
¼ cup honey
¼ cup vegetable oil

Ease the breakfast-time crunch with these light-as-air muffins. They come together in no time flat, store well in the pantry for several days, and taste absolutely delicious.

Preheat the oven to 400°F. Grease a 12-cup muffin pan.

In a medium bowl, combine the bran cereal, milk, and raisins. Let sit for 10 minutes.

In another bowl, whisk together the flour, baking soda, and salt.

In a large bowl, combine the egg, sour cream, honey, and oil. Stir in the bran mixture. Stir in the flour mixture until just combined. Do not overmix.

Divide the batter evenly among the prepared muffin cups, filling them about two-thirds full. Bake for 20 minutes, or until a wooden pick inserted in the center of a muffin comes out clean. Cool in the pan on a rack.

Makes 12

Per muffin: 181 calories, 4 g protein, 25 g carbohydrates, 10 g fat, 27 mg cholesterol, 3 g fiber, 290 mg sodium

Maple-Topped Muffins

Muffins

1½ cups unbleached all-purpose flour

½ cup chopped pecans

1½ teaspoons baking powder

½ teaspoon salt

¾ cup maple syrup

3 tablespoons butter, melted and cooled slightly

2 eggs

1½ teaspoons vanilla extract

Topping

2 tablespoons maple syrup

1 tablespoon packed brown sugar

½ teaspoon ground cinnamon

¼ teaspoon freshly ground nutmeg

Once called "sweetwater" by Native Americans, maple syrup provides the dominant flavor in these undeniably good muffins. Perfect for brunch, lunch, or snack.

To make the muffins: Preheat the oven to 400°F. Grease a 12-cup muffin pan.

In a medium bowl, combine the flour, pecans, baking powder, and salt.

In a large bowl, combine the maple syrup, butter, eggs, and vanilla extract. Stir in the flour mixture until just combined. Do not overmix.

Divide the batter evenly among the prepared muffin cups, filling them about two-thirds full.

To make the topping: In a small bowl, combine the maple syrup, brown sugar, cinnamon, and nutmeg. Evenly spoon over the muffin batter.

Bake for 10 minutes, or until a wooden pick inserted in the center of a muffin comes out clean. Cool on a rack for 5 minutes. Remove to the rack to cool completely.

Makes 12

Per muffin: 198 calories, 4 g protein, 31 g carbohydrates, 8 g fat, 44 mg cholesterol, 1 g fiber, 192 mg sodium

Wholesome Oat Muffins

1   cup + 2 tablespoons oats
1   cup buttermilk
1   cup unbleached all-
     purpose flour
1½ teaspoons baking
     powder
½   teaspoon baking soda
¼   teaspoon ground
     cinnamon
¼   teaspoon salt
⅓   cup vegetable oil
1   egg
⅓   cup packed brown sugar
1   teaspoon vanilla extract

These healthy bites are so delicious you will want them for breakfast every day. Make a double batch and freeze half for a quick breakfast treat.

Preheat the oven to 425°F. Grease a 12-cup muffin pan.

In a small bowl, combine 1 cup of the oats and the buttermilk. Let soak for 30 minutes.

In a medium bowl, combine the flour, baking powder, baking soda, cinnamon, and salt.

In a large bowl, stir together the oil, egg, brown sugar, and vanilla extract until well-blended. Stir in the oat mixture. Stir in the flour mixture until just combined. Do not overmix.

Divide the batter evenly among the prepared muffin cups, filling them about two-thirds full. Sprinkle the remaining 2 tablespoons oats over the muffins. Bake for 11 to 15 minutes, or until a wooden pick inserted in the center of a muffin comes out clean. Cool on a rack for 5 minutes. Remove to the rack to cool completely.

Makes 12
Per muffin: 192 calories, 5 g protein, 25 g carbohydrates, 8 g fat, 19 mg cholesterol, 2 g fiber, 176 mg sodium

Sour Cream Muffins

2 cups unbleached all-purpose flour

½ cup sugar

2½ teaspoons baking powder

½ teaspoon baking soda

½ teaspoon salt

1 cup dried cranberries or raisins

¾ cup milk

3 tablespoons vegetable oil

½ cup (4 ounces) sour cream

1 egg

1 teaspoon vanilla extract

Sour cream in muffins? Why not? Here, it replaces the usual buttermilk for a mellow flavor that nicely offsets the cranberries.

Preheat the oven to 400°F. Grease a 12-cup muffin pan.

In a medium bowl, combine the flour, sugar, baking powder, baking soda, and salt. Add the cranberries or raisins, and toss gently.

In a large bowl, combine the milk, oil, sour cream, egg, and vanilla extract. Stir in the flour mixture until just combined. Do not overmix.

Divide the batter evenly among the prepared muffin cups, filling them about two-thirds full. Bake for 12 to 15 minutes, or until a wooden pick inserted in the center of a muffin comes out clean. Cool on a rack for 5 minutes. Remove to the rack to cool completely.

Makes 12

Per muffin: 212 calories, 5 g protein, 36 g carbohydrates, 7 g fat, 24 mg cholesterol, 1 g fiber, 252 mg sodium

Zucchini Muffins

1⅓ cups unbleached all-purpose flour
1 teaspoon ground cinnamon
¾ teaspoon baking powder
½ teaspoon baking soda
½ teaspoon ground cloves
⅛ teaspoon salt
1½ cups shredded zucchini (about 1 large)
¼ cup milk
2 tablespoons vegetable oil
2 tablespoons honey
1 egg
⅔ cup sugar
1 teaspoon vanilla extract

Zucchini shreds fleck these healthful muffins—perfect for breakfast or an afternoon pick-me-up.

Preheat the oven to 350°F. Grease a 12-cup muffin pan.

In a medium bowl, combine the flour, cinnamon, baking powder, baking soda, cloves, and salt.

In a large bowl, stir together the zucchini, milk, oil, honey, egg, sugar, and vanilla extract. Stir in the flour mixture until just combined. Do not overmix.

Divide the batter evenly among the prepared muffin cups, filling them about two-thirds full. Bake for 12 to 15 minutes, or until a wooden pick inserted in the center of a muffin comes out clean. Cool on a rack for 5 minutes. Remove to the rack to cool completely.

Makes 12
Per muffin: 133 calories, 2 g protein, 26 g carbohydrates, 3 g fat, 18 mg cholesterol, 1 g fiber, 108 mg sodium

Raspberry Muffins

1½ cups unbleached all-purpose flour

2 teaspoons baking powder

1 teaspoon baking soda

¼ teaspoon salt

¾ cup buttermilk

¼ cup butter, melted and cooled slightly

1 egg

⅓ cup sugar

1 teaspoon grated lemon peel

1 cup raspberries

Nothing elaborate here—just an uncommonly good muffin that showcases fresh raspberries. Happy noshing!

Preheat the oven to 400°F. Grease a 12-cup muffin pan.

In a medium bowl, combine the flour, baking powder, baking soda, and salt.

In a large bowl, stir together the buttermilk, butter, egg, sugar, and lemon peel until well-blended. Stir in the flour mixture until just combined. Do not overmix. Gently fold in the raspberries.

Divide the batter evenly among the prepared muffin cups, filling them about two-thirds full. Bake for 12 to 15 minutes, or until a wooden pick inserted in the center of a muffin comes out clean. Cool on a rack for 5 minutes. Remove to the rack to cool completely.

Makes 12

Per muffin: 135 calories, 3 g protein, 20 g carbohydrates, 5 g fat, 30 mg cholesterol, 1 g fiber, 283 mg sodium

Sugared Ginger Muffins

1½ cups unbleached all-purpose flour

2 teaspoons baking powder

1 teaspoon baking soda

½ teaspoon salt

¾ cup buttermilk

¼ cup butter, melted and cooled slightly

1 egg

⅓ cup granulated sugar

2 tablespoons chopped crystallized ginger

1 tablespoon coarse sugar (optional)

These tender muffins get their sweetness from crystallized ginger and a sprinkling of coarse sugar.

Preheat the oven to 400°F. Grease a 12-cup muffin pan.

In a medium bowl, combine the flour, baking powder, baking soda, and salt.

In a large bowl, stir together the buttermilk, butter, egg, granulated sugar, and ginger until well-blended. Stir in the flour mixture until just combined. Do not overmix.

Divide the batter evenly among the prepared muffin cups, filling them about two-thirds full. Evenly sprinkle the batter with the coarse sugar (if using). Bake for 12 to 15 minutes, or until a wooden pick inserted in the center of a muffin comes out clean. Cool on a rack for 5 minutes. Remove to the rack to cool completely.

Makes 12

Per muffin: 130 calories, 4 g protein, 18 g carbohydrates, 5 g fat, 30 mg cholesterol, 1 g fiber, 332 mg sodium

Date and Almond Laced Muffins

- 2 **cups unbleached all-purpose flour**
- 2 **teaspoons baking powder**
- 1 **teaspoon ground cinnamon**
- ½ **teaspoon baking soda**
- ½ **teaspoon salt**
- ¼ **teaspoon ground cloves**
- ½ **cup pitted and finely chopped dates**
- ¼ **cup slivered almonds, toasted**
- ¾ **cup milk**
- ¾ **cup orange marmalade**
- ¼ **cup vegetable oil**
- 1 **egg**
- 2 **tablespoons granulated sugar**
- ½ **teaspoon grated orange peel**
- 2 **tablespoons cinnamon sugar**

Orange marmalade, a preserve containing pieces of citrus rind, is the sweetener in this unique recipe. Tasters gave it an enthusiastic thumbs up. We're sure you will, too.

Preheat the oven to 425°F. Grease a 12-cup muffin pan.

In a medium bowl, combine the flour, baking powder, cinnamon, baking soda, salt, and cloves. Add the dates and almonds. Toss gently.

In a large bowl, stir together the milk, marmalade, oil, egg, granulated sugar, and orange peel until well-blended. Stir in the flour mixture until just combined. Do not overmix.

Divide the batter evenly among the prepared muffin cups, filling them about two-thirds full. Evenly sprinkle the cinnamon sugar over the muffin batter. Bake for 12 to 15 minutes, or until a wooden pick inserted in the center of a muffin comes out clean. Cool on a rack for 5 minutes. Remove to the rack to cool completely.

Makes 12

Per muffin: 251 calories, 5 g protein, 42 g carbohydrates, 9 g fat, 20 mg cholesterol, 3 g fiber, 241 mg sodium

Orange–Poppy Seed Muffins

2 cups unbleached all-purpose flour

3 tablespoons grated orange peel

3 tablespoons poppy seeds

1 teaspoon baking powder

½ teaspoon baking soda

½ teaspoon salt

½ cup butter, at room temperature

¾ cup sugar

2 eggs

1 cup buttermilk

Often the tastiest foods come in tiny packages. Here poppy seeds, which measure less than $\frac{1}{16}$" in diameter, offer up tons of crunch and nutty flavor. You'll earn rave reviews with these creations.

Preheat the oven to 400°F. Grease a 12-cup muffin pan.

In a medium bowl, combine the flour, orange peel, poppy seeds, baking powder, baking soda, and salt.

In a large bowl, with an electric mixer on medium speed, beat the butter and sugar for 3 minutes, or until light and fluffy. Beat in the eggs and buttermilk. Stir in the flour mixture until just combined. Do not overmix.

Divide the batter evenly among the prepared muffin cups, filling them about two-thirds full. Bake for 12 to 15 minutes, or until a wooden pick inserted in the center of a muffin comes out clean. Cool on a rack for 5 minutes. Remove to the rack to cool completely.

Makes 12

Per muffin: 233 calories, 5 g protein, 31 g carbohydrates, 11 g fat, 59 mg cholesterol, 1 g fiber, 298 mg sodium

Peach Muffins

2 cups unbleached all-purpose flour

2½ teaspoons baking powder

¼ teaspoon salt

⅛ teaspoon allspice

½ cup chopped dried peaches, cherries, or mixed fruit

¼ cup shredded coconut

1 cup milk

¼ cup vegetable oil

1 egg

⅓ cup packed brown sugar

1 tablespoon finely chopped crystallized ginger

Peach pie, peach preserves, yes—but peach muffins? Sure thing. In this fuss-free recipe, dried peaches ensure vibrant flavor while crystallized ginger adds zing.

Preheat the oven to 400°F. Grease a 12-cup muffin pan.

In a medium bowl, combine the flour, baking powder, salt, and allspice. Stir in the peaches, cherries, or mixed fruit and the coconut.

In a large bowl, stir together the milk, oil, egg, and brown sugar until well-blended. Stir in the flour mixture until just combined. Do not overmix. Stir in the ginger.

Divide the batter evenly among the prepared muffin cups, filling them about two-thirds full. Bake for 12 to 15 minutes, or until a wooden pick inserted in the center of a muffin comes out clean. Cool on a rack for 5 minutes. Remove to the rack to cool completely.

Makes 12

Per muffin: 170 calories, 4 g protein, 25 g carbohydrates, 7 g fat, 21 mg cholesterol, 1 g fiber, 149 mg sodium

THE QUICKEST
BREADS AND
CAKES

Orange-Blueberry Loaf

1 cup blueberries

2 tablespoons + 1¾ cups unbleached all-purpose flour

¼ cup cornmeal

1½ teaspoons baking powder

½ teaspoon baking soda

½ teaspoon salt

6 tablespoons butter, at room temperature

¾ cup sugar

1 egg

½ cup orange juice

2 teaspoons grated orange peel

Cornmeal adds a slight crunch to this tender quick bread studded with blueberries and seasoned with lively orange flavors.

Preheat the oven to 350°F. Grease and flour one 8½" x 4½" loaf pan.

In a small bowl, toss together the blueberries and 2 tablespoons flour.

In a medium bowl, combine the cornmeal, baking powder, baking soda, salt, and the remaining 1¾ cups flour.

In a large bowl, with an electric mixer on high speed, beat the butter and sugar for 3 minutes, or until light and fluffy. Add the egg and beat well. Beat in the orange juice and orange peel. Add the flour mixture and, with the mixer on low speed, beat until well-blended. Stir in the blueberries. Spread into the prepared pan. Bake for 55 to 65 minutes, or until a wooden pick inserted in the center comes out clean. Cool on a rack for 5 minutes. Remove from the pan and cool completely on the rack.

Makes 12 servings

Per serving: 203 calories, 4 g protein, 33 g carbohydrates, 7 g fat, 35 mg cholesterol, 1 g fiber, 269 mg sodium

Coconut Chocolate Cake

1½ cups unbleached all-purpose flour

½ cup unsweetened cocoa powder

½ teaspoon baking powder

½ teaspoon baking soda

½ teaspoon salt

½ cup butter, at room temperature

¾ cup sugar

2 eggs

1 cup (8 ounces) sour cream

¾ cup bittersweet or semisweet chocolate chips

½ cup flaked coconut, toasted

So delicious in candy, the classic marriage of chocolate and coconut is outstanding in this rich cake. Perfect with cappuccino or flavored coffee.

Preheat the oven to 350°F. Grease and flour one 8½" x 4½" loaf pan.

In a medium bowl, combine the flour, cocoa powder, baking powder, baking soda, and salt.

In a large bowl, with an electric mixer on high speed, beat the butter and sugar for 3 minutes, or until light and fluffy. Add the eggs and beat well. Beat in the sour cream. Add the flour mixture and, with the mixer on low speed, beat until well-blended. Stir in the chocolate chips and coconut. Spread into the prepared pan. Bake for 55 to 65 minutes, or until a wooden pick inserted in the center comes out clean. Cool on a rack for 5 minutes. Remove from the pan and cool completely on the rack.

Makes 16 servings

Per serving: 236 calories, 5 g protein, 26 g carbohydrates, 14 g fat, 50 mg cholesterol, 1 g fiber, 207 mg sodium

Lemon-Anise Tea Cake

2   **cups unbleached all-purpose flour**

½   **teaspoon baking powder**

½   **teaspoon baking soda**

½   **teaspoon salt**

½   **cup butter, at room temperature**

¾   **cup sugar**

2   **eggs**

1   **cup buttermilk**

3   **tablespoons grated lemon peel**

1   **tablespoon anise seed, ground**

This lemon loaf is flavored with ground anise seed which imparts a sweet, slightly licorice taste. Serve with whipped cream cheese or raspberry all-fruit spread.

Preheat the oven to 350°F. Grease and flour one 8½" x 4½" loaf pan.

In a medium bowl, combine the flour, baking powder, baking soda, and salt.

In a large bowl, with an electric mixer on high speed, beat the butter and sugar for 3 minutes, or until light and fluffy. Add the eggs and beat well. Beat in the buttermilk. Add the flour mixture and, with the mixer on low speed, beat until well-blended. Stir in the lemon peel and anise seed. Spread into the prepared pan. Bake for 55 to 65 minutes, or until a wooden pick inserted in the center comes out clean. Cool on a rack for 5 minutes. Remove from the pan and cool completely on the rack.

Makes 12 servings

Per serving: 223 calories, 5 g protein, 31 g carbohydrates, 10 g fat, 59 mg cholesterol, 1 g fiber, 281 mg sodium

---

COOKING TIP

The easiest way to grind seeds, such as anise or fennel, is to place the seeds in a clean coffee grinder and process until fine. If you do not have a grinder, use a mortar and pestle or place the seeds in a resealable food storage bag, seal, and crush with a rolling pin.

Fruit-Studded Coffee Cake

3 cups unbleached all-purpose flour

1½ cups granulated sugar

2 teaspoons baking powder

1 teaspoon baking soda

½ teaspoon salt

2 teaspoons grated orange peel

¾ cup cold butter

1½ cups (12 ounces) sour cream

3 eggs, slightly beaten

2 tablespoons orange juice

1 teaspoon vanilla extract

¾ cup mixed dried fruits, chopped

2 tablespoons confectioners' sugar (optional)

Unlike the dense fruit cakes of the holiday season, this light cake is loaded with freshly dried fruits such as raisins, cranberries, and cherries.

Preheat the oven to 350°F. Grease and flour a 12-cup Bundt pan.

In a large bowl, combine the flour, granulated sugar, baking powder, baking soda, salt, and orange peel. Using a pastry blender or two knives, cut in the butter until the mixture resembles coarse crumbs. Stir in the sour cream, eggs, orange juice, and vanilla extract. Mix until well-blended. Fold in the dried fruits.

Place in the prepared pan and bake for 1 hour, or until a wooden pick inserted in the center comes out clean. Cool on a rack for 10 minutes. Invert onto the rack and cool completely. Dust with confectioners' sugar (if using).

Makes 16 servings
Per serving: 318 calories, 5 g protein, 44 g carbohydrates, 14 g fat, 73 mg cholesterol, 1 g fiber, 316 mg sodium

Marble Pound Cake

4 ounces unsweetened chocolate

3½ cups unbleached all-purpose flour

2 teaspoons baking powder

1 teaspoon baking soda

½ teaspoon salt

1 cup butter, at room temperature

2 cups sugar

1 cup (8 ounces) sour cream

4 eggs

1½ teaspoons almond extract

This classic marble cake is baked in a Bundt pan to eliminate the need for frosting. If you crave a very decadent cake, drizzle with a bit of warmed fudge sauce.

Preheat the oven to 350°F. Grease a 12-cup Bundt pan.

Melt the chocolate in a small saucepan over low heat. Remove from the heat and let cool.

In a medium bowl, combine the flour, baking powder, baking soda, and salt.

In a large bowl, with an electric mixer on medium speed, beat the butter and sugar for 3 minutes, or until light and fluffy. Add the sour cream, eggs, and almond extract and beat well. Add the flour mixture and, with the mixer on low speed, beat just until blended.

Place 2½ cups of the batter in a small bowl and set aside.

Stir the cooled chocolate into the remaining batter. Spoon about two-thirds of the chocolate batter into the prepared pan. Spread the plain batter over the chocolate in the pan. Top with the remaining one-third of the chocolate batter. Using a butter knife, swirl the plain batter into the chocolate to marbleize.

Bake for 1 hour, or until a wooden pick inserted in the center comes out clean. Cool on a rack for 10 minutes. Invert onto the rack and cool completely.

Makes 16 servings

Per serving: 287 calories, 5 g protein, 37 g carbohydrates, 14 g fat, 61 mg cholesterol, 1 g fiber, 233 mg sodium

Espresso Ring

2 tablespoons + 2½ cups sugar

4 cups unbleached all-purpose flour

¼ cup finely ground rich coffee, such as espresso or French roast

1 tablespoon baking powder

½ teaspoon salt

1 cup butter, at room temperature

½ cup (4 ounces) sour cream

6 eggs

1 tablespoon vanilla extract

½ cup milk

Loaded with rich espresso flecks, this sweet cake is delicious for dessert or a mid-afternoon pick-me-up.

Preheat the oven to 350°F. Grease a 12-cup Bundt pan and sprinkle with the 2 tablespoons sugar.

In a medium bowl, combine the flour, coffee, baking powder, and salt.

In a large bowl, with an electric mixer on medium speed, beat the butter and remaining 2½ cups sugar for 3 minutes, or until light and fluffy. Add the sour cream, eggs, and vanilla extract and beat well. Add the flour mixture and milk. With the mixer on low speed, beat until well-blended.

Place in the prepared pan and bake for 1 hour, or until a wooden pick inserted in the center comes out clean. Cool on a rack for 10 minutes. Invert onto the rack and cool completely.

Makes 16 servings
Per serving: 394 calories, 7 g protein, 58 g carbohydrates, 16 g fat, 116 mg cholesterol, 0 g fiber, 299 mg sodium

Gingerbread

1½ cups unbleached all-purpose flour

1½ teaspoons pumpkin pie spice

½ teaspoon baking powder

½ teaspoon baking soda

¼ teaspoon salt

½ cup butter

¼ cup packed brown sugar

1 egg

½ cup light molasses

Served with a dollop of whipped cream or a few tablespoons of hard sauce, this classic cake is lovely for tea or dessert.

Preheat the oven to 350°F. Grease a 9" x 9" baking pan.

In a medium bowl, combine the flour, pumpkin pie spice, baking powder, baking soda, and salt.

In a large bowl, with an electric mixer on medium speed, beat the butter and brown sugar for 3 minutes, or until light and fluffy. Add the egg and molasses and beat well. Add the flour mixture and, with the mixer on low speed, beat until well-blended.

Bake for 35 to 40 minutes, or until a wooden pick inserted in the center comes out clean. Cool completely on a rack.

Makes 9 servings

Per serving: 283 calories, 5 g protein, 41 g carbohydrates, 12 g fat, 53 mg cholesterol, 1 g fiber, 283 mg sodium

Chocolate Zucchini Cake

2¼ cups unbleached all-purpose flour

½ cup unsweetened cocoa powder

2 teaspoons baking powder

1 teaspoon baking soda

½ teaspoon salt

⅔ cup vegetable oil

½ cup buttermilk

3 eggs

1½ cups sugar

3 cups shredded zucchini (about 3 medium)

No one will notice that this cake is loaded with healthy zucchini. For an even richer chocolate flavor, sprinkle 1 cup of chocolate chips over the warm cake and spread evenly to frost. Cool completely before cutting.

Preheat the oven to 350°F. Grease a 13" x 9" baking pan.

In a medium bowl, combine the flour, cocoa powder, baking powder, baking soda, and salt.

In a large bowl, combine the oil, buttermilk, eggs, sugar, and zucchini. Stir in the flour mixture until just blended. Place in the prepared pan. Bake for 30 minutes, or until a wooden pick inserted in the center comes out clean. Cool completely on a rack.

Makes 16 servings

Per serving: 254 calories, 6 g protein, 35 g carbohydrates, 12 g fat, 41 mg cholesterol, 1 g fiber, 226 mg sodium

Bananas Foster Squares

2½ cups unbleached all-purpose flour

1 teaspoon baking powder

½ teaspoon baking soda

½ teaspoon salt

¾ cup butter, at room temperature

1 cup firmly packed brown sugar

½ cup (4 ounces) sour cream

1 egg

½ teaspoon rum extract

2 very ripe bananas, mashed (1 cup)

1 package (10 ounces) butterscotch chips

This sweet, light cake highlights the flavor combination of the dessert Bananas Foster. Bananas, rum, and brown sugar are classic flavors—serve with a scoop of vanilla ice cream for an even more authentic rendition.

Preheat the oven to 350°F. Grease a 13" x 9" baking pan.

In a medium bowl, combine the flour, baking powder, baking soda, and salt.

In a large bowl, with an electric mixer on medium speed, beat the butter and brown sugar for 3 minutes, or until light and fluffy. Add the sour cream, egg, and rum extract and beat well. Add the mashed bananas and the flour mixture. With the mixer on low speed, beat until well-blended.

Place in the prepared pan. Bake for 30 minutes, or until a wooden pick inserted in the center comes out clean. Place on a wire rack to cool. While still hot, sprinkle the chips over the cake. As they melt, spread with a spatula to ice the cake.

Makes 16 servings

Per serving: 344 calories, 5 g protein, 47 g carbohydrates, 18 g fat, 41 mg cholesterol, 2 g fiber, 245 mg sodium

Apricot Squares

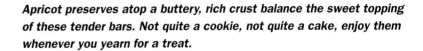

- 2½ cups unbleached all-purpose flour
- ½ teaspoon baking powder
- ½ teaspoon salt
- ¾ cup butter
- 1½ cups packed brown sugar
- 1 jar (12 ounces) apricot preserves
- 2 eggs
- 1 teaspoon vanilla extract
- 1 tablespoon confectioners' sugar

Apricot preserves atop a buttery, rich crust balance the sweet topping of these tender bars. Not quite a cookie, not quite a cake, enjoy them whenever you yearn for a treat.

Preheat the oven to 325°F. Grease a 13" x 9" baking pan.

In a small bowl, combine ½ cup of the flour, the baking powder, and salt. Set aside.

In a medium bowl, with an electric mixer on medium speed, beat the butter and ½ cup of the brown sugar until light and creamy. Gradually add the remaining 2 cups flour, beating with the mixer on low speed, just until the mixture resembles coarse crumbs. Press into the prepared pan. Spread the preserves over the butter mixture.

In another medium bowl, with an electric mixer on high speed, beat the eggs and remaining 1 cup brown sugar until thick. Beat in the vanilla extract. Gradually add the flour mixture, beating on low speed until just combined. Spread over the preserves.

Bake for 40 minutes, or until lightly browned. Place on a rack to cool completely. Dust with the confectioners' sugar before serving.

Makes 24 servings
Per serving: 195 calories, 2 g protein, 33 g carbohydrates, 7 g fat, 34 mg cholesterol, 0 g fiber, 129 mg sodium

Carrot Cake

- 2½ cups unbleached all-purpose flour
- ½ teaspoon baking soda
- ½ teaspoon ground cardamom
- ½ teaspoon ground ginger
- ¼ teaspoon salt
- 1 cup vegetable oil
- ½ cup apple juice
- 1½ cups granulated sugar
- 2 eggs
- 3 cups shredded carrots (about 3 large)
- 4 ounces Neufchâtel cream cheese
- ⅓ cup confectioners' sugar

This favorite cake is simple to prepare—it is baked and served in the same pan. If time does not allow for preparing the icing, sprinkle with confectioners' sugar for a delicious variation.

Preheat the oven to 350°F. Grease a 13" x 9" baking pan.

In a medium bowl, combine the flour, baking soda, cardamom, ginger, and salt.

In a large bowl, combine the oil, apple juice, granulated sugar, eggs, and carrots. Stir in the flour mixture until just blended. Spread into the prepared pan. Bake for 30 minutes, or until a wooden pick inserted in the center comes out clean. Cool completely on a wire rack.

Meanwhile, in a small bowl, with an electric mixer on medium speed, beat the cream cheese and confectioners' sugar until smooth. Spread over the cooled cake.

Makes 16 servings

Per serving: 318 calories, 5 g protein, 41 g carbohydrates, 17 g fat, 33 mg cholesterol, 1 g fiber, 86 mg sodium

Quick Chocolate-Raspberry Torte

4 squares (1 ounce each) semisweet chocolate

½ cup butter

½ cup raspberry preserves

⅓ cup sugar

2 eggs, at room temperature

2 tablespoons raspberry liqueur or orange juice

1 cup cake flour

1 teaspoon baking powder

½ cup chocolate fudge topping

Use the microwave to bake this cake and it's ready in just 15 minutes. Perfect for guests.

Grease an 8" (1½-quart) round microwaveable baking dish. Place wax paper on the bottom of the dish and grease the paper.

Place the chocolate and butter in a microwaveable bowl. Microwave on high for 4 minutes, or until the chocolate and butter are melted.

In a medium bowl, stir together the preserves, sugar, eggs, liqueur or orange juice, flour, and baking powder until just combined. Stir in the melted chocolate mixture. Pour into the prepared dish. Cover with vented plastic wrap.

Place the dish on an inverted saucer in a microwave oven. Microwave on high for 6 minutes until the center is slightly wet. Let stand for 3 minutes. Invert onto a serving plate and spread the top of the cake with the topping.

Makes 8 servings

Per serving: 332 calories, 4 g protein, 43 g carbohydrates, 18 g fat, 86 mg cholesterol, 1 g fiber, 203 mg sodium

Almond-Cocoa Angel Cake

Cocoa Cake

½ cup unbleached all-purpose flour, sifted

2 tablespoons unsweetened cocoa powder, sifted

⅛ teaspoon salt

6 tablespoons + ½ cup sugar

6 egg whites, at room temperature

1 teaspoon cream of tartar

1 teaspoon almond extract

Fruit Sauce

¼ cup orange juice

1 tablespoon cornstarch

1 tablespoon sugar

2 peaches, pitted and sliced

½ pint raspberries

Low-fat and yet so chocolatey, this light cake is made extra special with a peach and raspberry sauce. Use different fruit combinations, such as apricots and strawberries or nectarines and blueberries, for a nice change of pace.

Preheat the oven to 350°F.

To make the cocoa cake: In a medium bowl, combine the flour, cocoa powder, salt, and 6 tablespoons of the sugar.

In a large bowl, with an electric mixer on medium speed, beat the egg whites until foamy. Add the cream of tartar and almond extract. Increase the mixer speed to high. Gradually add the remaining ½ cup sugar and beat until stiff, glossy peaks form and the sugar dissolves.

Fold the flour mixture, one-third at a time, into the beaten whites. Place in an ungreased 9" x 5" loaf pan and bake for 25 minutes, or until a wooden pick inserted in the center comes out clean. Turn upside down on a rack and cool for 30 minutes.

To make the fruit sauce: In a small saucepan, whisk together the orange juice, cornstarch, and sugar. Bring to a boil over medium heat. Boil for 2 minutes, or until thickened. Remove from the heat and stir in the peaches and raspberries. Let cool.

When the cake has cooled, using a knife, release the sides of the cake. Remove to a serving plate. Slice into 16 slices.

To serve, place 2 slices of cake onto each of 8 dessert plates. Top the slices with the peach mixture.

Makes 8 servings
Per serving: 256 calories, 6 g protein, 48 g carbohydrates, 2 g fat, 0 mg cholesterol, 2 g fiber, 173 mg sodium

German Chocolate Cake

1½ cups unbleached all-purpose flour

½ cup unsweetened cocoa powder

½ cup sugar

1 tablespoon baking powder

¼ teaspoon salt

½ cup butter

1 egg

⅔ cup milk

2 teaspoons vanilla extract

½ cup shredded coconut, toasted

½ cup pecan halves, toasted

½ cup caramel topping

Traditionally a two-tiered layer cake, this simple version is ready in no time and is just as sweet and delicious as an elaborate cake.

Preheat the oven to 350°F. Grease and flour a 9" round cake pan.

In a large bowl, combine the flour, cocoa powder, sugar, baking powder, and salt. Using a pastry blender or two knives, cut in the butter until the mixture resembles coarse crumbs. Stir in the egg, milk, and vanilla extract. Mix until well-blended.

Place in the prepared pan and bake for 15 minutes, or until a wooden pick inserted in the center comes out clean. Cool on a rack for 10 minutes. Invert onto a serving plate.

In a small bowl, combine the coconut, pecans, and caramel topping. Spread onto the top of the cake.

Makes 10 servings

Per serving: 299 calories, 5 g protein, 37 g carbohydrates, 16 g fat, 43 mg cholesterol, 1 g fiber, 300 mg sodium

Mint Chocolate Cake

4   eggs, separated

½   cup + 2 tablespoons butter

1   cup sugar

2   teaspoons vanilla extract

1   cup unbleached all-purpose flour

1   package (10 ounces) mint chocolate chips, melted and cooled

¼   cup milk

This dense, rich chocolate cake is actually quite delicious as is, but for a special occasion serve each slice with a dollop of lightly whipped cream.

Preheat the oven to 350°F. Grease a 9" springform pan.

In a large bowl, with an electric mixer on high speed, beat the egg whites until stiff peaks form. Set aside.

In another large bowl, using the same beaters, beat the sugar and ½ cup of the butter at medium speed for 3 minutes, or until light and fluffy. Add the egg yolks and vanilla extract and beat well. Beat in the flour. Add the melted chocolate chips and milk and, with the mixer on low speed, beat until well-blended.

Using a wooden spoon, stir in 1 cup of the beaten egg whites. Fold in the remaining whites. Spread into the prepared pan.

Bake for 45 minutes, or until a wooden pick inserted into the center comes out clean. Cool on a rack for 15 minutes; remove the cake from the pan and cool completely.

Makes 12 servings
Per serving: 342 calories, 6 g protein, 41 g carbohydrates, 19 g fat, 100 mg cholesterol, 0 g fiber, 147 mg sodium

Simple Chocolate Cake

1   **cup unbleached all-purpose flour**

½   **cup sugar**

3   **tablespoons unsweetened cocoa powder**

1   **teaspoon ground cinnamon**

1   **teaspoon baking soda**

¼   **teaspoon salt**

8   **ounces vanilla yogurt**

2   **tablespoons vegetable oil**

1   **teaspoon vanilla extract**

2   **eggs, separated**

Light and delicate, this lower-fat cake has a surprisingly rich chocolate flavor. Serve with frozen yogurt and pourable all-fruit for special occasions.

Preheat the oven to 350°F. Grease an 8" or 9" round cake pan.

In a medium bowl, combine the flour, sugar, cocoa powder, cinnamon, baking soda, and salt.

In a large bowl, combine the yogurt, oil, vanilla extract, and egg yolks.

In a medium bowl, with an electric mixer on high speed, beat the egg whites until stiff peaks form.

Stir the flour mixture into the yogurt mixture until just blended. Fold the egg whites into the flour mixture. Pour into the prepared pan.

Bake for 35 minutes, or until a wooden pick inserted in the center comes out clean. Cool on a rack for 5 minutes. Remove to the rack to cool completely.

Makes 12 servings

Per serving: 152 calories, 4 g protein, 24 g carbohydrates, 5 g fat, 43 mg cholesterol, 1 g fiber, 212 mg sodium

Index

C

CONVERSION CHART

These equivalents have been slightly rounded to make measuring easier.

Volume Measurements

U.S.	Imperial	Metric
¼ tsp	–	1 ml
½ tsp	–	2 ml
1 tsp	–	5 ml
1 Tbsp	–	15 ml
2 Tbsp (1 oz)	1 fl oz	30 ml
¼ cup (2 oz)	2 fl oz	60 ml
⅓ cup (3 oz)	3 fl oz	80 ml
½ cup (4 oz)	4 fl oz	120 ml
⅔ cup (5 oz)	5 fl oz	160 ml
¾ cup (6 oz)	6 fl oz	180 ml
1 cup (8 oz)	8 fl oz	240 ml

Weight Measurements

U.S.	Metric
1 oz	30 g
2 oz	60 g
4 oz (¼ lb)	115 g
5 oz (⅓ lb)	145 g
6 oz	170 g
7 oz	200 g
8 oz (½ lb)	230 g
10 oz	285 g
12 oz (¾ lb)	340 g
14 oz	400 g
16 oz (1 lb)	455 g
2.2 lb	1 kg

Length Measurements

U.S.	Metric
¼"	0.6 cm
½"	1.25 cm
1"	2.5 cm
2"	5 cm
4"	11 cm
6"	15 cm
8"	20 cm
10"	25 cm
12" (1')	30 cm

Pan Sizes

U.S.	Metric
8" cake pan	20 × 4 cm sandwich or cake tin
9" cake pan	23 × 3.5 cm sandwich or cake tin
11" × 7" baking pan	28 × 18 cm baking tin
13" × 9" baking pan	32.5 × 23 cm baking tin
15" × 10" baking pan	38 × 25.5 cm baking tin (Swiss roll tin)
2 qt rectangular baking dish	30 × 19 cm baking dish
1½ qt baking dish	1.5 liter baking dish
2 qt baking dish	2 liter baking dish
9" pie plate	22 × 4 or 23 × 4 cm pie plate
7" or 8" springform pan	18 or 20 cm springform or loose-bottom cake tin
9" × 5" loaf pan	23 × 13 cm or 2 lb narrow loaf tin or pâté tin

Temperatures

Fahrenheit	Centigrade	Gas
140°	60°	–
160°	70°	–
180°	80°	–
225°	110°	–
250°	120°	½
300°	150°	2
325°	160°	3
350°	180°	4
375°	190°	5
400°	200°	6
450°	230°	8
500°	260°	–